CW01511085

MANAGING THE OUTSOURCING RELATIONSHIP

KIM LANGFIELD-SMITH BEc (Syd), MEc (Macq) PhD (Mon) FCPA is Professor of Accounting, and Head of the School of Business at La Trobe University. She previously held positions at Monash University, the University of Melbourne and the University of Tasmania. From 1999 to 2001 she was President of the Accounting Association of Australia and New Zealand (AAANZ). Kim's research interests are in management accounting, and she has published in accounting, management and psychology in many international journals.

DAVID SMITH BCom (Hons) (La Trobe) is a Lecturer in the Department of Accounting and Management at La Trobe University where he is also undertaking a PhD. He was previously employed in the Department of Accounting and Finance at Monash University. His research interests are in management accounting.

CAROLYN STRINGER MBus (Acc), BBus (Acc) Hons, CMA, ASA is a Lecturer of Accounting at University of Otago, Dunedin, New Zealand. She has previously held a position at Monash University. Carolyn's research interests are in management and internal control.

THE AUSTRALIAN CENTRE FOR MANAGEMENT ACCOUNTING DEVELOPMENT (ACMAD) is a network driven and financed by a membership of almost 100 organisations and universities. Its mission is to stimulate and facilitate learning about the innovative management of organisational resources. This series is one expression of its mission. ACMAD welcomes inquiries. Further information about the Centre is provided on its website at: www.ace.unsw.edu.au/acmad

THE INSTITUTE OF CHARTERED ACCOUNTANTS IN AUSTRALIA believes that the Strategic Resource Management series will contribute to the clarification of a range of significant issues facing managers and business professionals in the future. The practical insights and distinctive perspectives offered will greatly benefit our members and will add value to anyone who is a strategic business thinker.

Series editor

Professor William Birkett is Professor of Accounting at the University of New South Wales, and Associate Dean—Development in its Faculty of Commerce and Economics. For the past 10 years, he has been Director of the Australian Centre for Management Accounting Development, which networks close to 100 organisations moving towards best practice through innovations in resource management. He is the author or co-author of 20 monographs and over 30 articles in research and practitioner-oriented journals. Professor Birkett has researched professional competences as organisational resources in Australia and internationally, and worked with the Financial and Management Accounting Committee of the International Federation of Accountants to produce the authoritative document that has redefined Management Accounting as Strategic Resource Management.

Other books in the series:

Controls in Strategic Supplier Relationships
Suresh Cuganesan, Michael Briers and Wai Fong Chua

Harnessing Organisational Resources: Purchasing Cards in Action
Clinton Free, Michael Briers and Peter Luckett

Innovative Management Accounting: Insights from practice
Maria Barbera, Jane Baxter and William Birkett

Organisational Learning and Management Accounting Systems:
A study of local government
Louise Kloot, Maria Italia, Judy Oliver and Albie Brooks

Shareholder Value Demystified: An explanation of methodolgies and use
Maria Barbera and Rodney Coyte

STRATEGIC RESOURCE MANAGEMENT

Kim Langfield-Smith | David Smith | Carolyn Stringer

MANAGING THE OUTSOURCING RELATIONSHIP

Chartered Accountants

A UNSW Press book

Published by
University of New South Wales Press Ltd
UNSW SYDNEY NSW 2052
AUSTRALIA
www.unswpress.com.au

© ACMAD 2000
First published 2000

This book is copyright. Apart from any fair dealing for the purpose
of private study, research, criticism or review, as permitted under the
Copyright Act, no part may be reproduced by any process without
written permission. Inquiries should be addressed to the publisher.

National Library of Australia
Cataloguing-in-Publication entry:

Langfield-Smith, Kim.
Managing the outsourcing relationship.

Bibliography.
ISBN 0 86840 771 2.

1. Contracting out — Australia — Management. 2. Contracting
out — Australia — Case studies. I. Stringer, Carolyn. II. Smith,
David Alan. III. Title. (Series: Strategic resource management.)

658.723

Printer Brown Prior Anderson

CONTENTS

STRATEGIC RESOURCE MANAGEMENT

Organisations are devices for creating value through the effective use of resources. While they need to create value for all contributors of resources, a premium is placed on value creation for customers and shareholders. After all, an organisation is unlikely to be able to offer inducements to other resource contributors if it does not provide value to its customers. Also, shareholders are aware that failure in value creation for customers will be reflected in the value that they can receive. Value creation for customers and shareholders, then, is broadly regarded as the litmus test for judging organisational effectiveness.

Value creation by organisations takes place against a backdrop of fast moving competition in resource and service markets, and increasingly rapid shifts in the value expectations of customers. Under these conditions it is insufficient to meet or beat the competition with present service offerings; new service offerings have to be invented and made competitive, as previous offerings cease to be serviceable and are thus devalued.

As service offerings change, so will the materials, technologies, skills and processes that are needed to produce them. New service offerings require different constellations of resources and new relationships with new resource contributors.

An organisation's *strategies* define how it proposes to create value for customers in terms of its service offerings over the immediate period and the opportunities it seeks over a longer term. Whether or not an organisation will be successful in these endeavours will depend on its *capabilities* for doing so.

Strategies, then, have to deal with both the known (the creation of value through present service offerings) and the unknown (the invention of service offerings that will create value in an as yet unknown future). And capabilities need to sustain both the organisation's present effectiveness in offering services and its future renewal by capitalising on opportunities as they emerge.

An organisation's success in strategy realisation or renewal will be dependent on its effectiveness and creativity in managing resources. This places a premium on *strategic resource management* and on new ways of understanding organisational resources, resourcing and resourcefulness. What are an organisation's resources, what forms do they take and how can they be used effectively and not wasted? What constellations of resources constitute strategic capabilities, useable now in meeting the competition and converting possibilities into future opportunities? And what strategic capabilities are sufficiently distinctive to constitute the core competences underlying an organisation's continuing identity?

These questions are answered in the Strategic Resource Management Series. Each volume will address them in relation to particular subject matter, drawing on relevant theories and providing illustrations from contemporary organisational practice.

PREFACE

The practice of outsourcing is a global phenomenon that has increased over the past twenty years, and there are indications that it will increase further in this new century. While much has been written about 'what should be outsourced', little has been written about the important aspects of managing the relationship between the firm and the outsourcer, and how control can be achieved when critical organisational functions are outsourced.

The purpose of this study is to report on the outsourcing experiences of four Australian organisations—a manufacturer of steel, an electricity marketer, a local government council, and an electricity network supplier. The study addresses the following questions: What are the important issues that must be managed within an outsourcing relationship? Is it more difficult to control an outsourced activity, compared to an in-house activity?

The decision processes and experiences of the four Australian organisations provide the background to addressing these questions.

1

INTRODUCTION

Massive growth in outsourcing, in both public and private sector organisations, occurred during the 1990s. Not only have businesses outsourced ancillary functions such as cleaning and catering, but more critical areas of the business, such as information technology, manufacturing, and human resource management have been contracted out to third parties.

The practice of outsourcing is an international phenomenon. Digital Corporation in the United States has outsourced its entire labour force and much of its production management to a labour hire firm. The global clothing manufacturer Benetton is little more than a shell, having outsourced its product design, manufacturing, and merchandising to contractors. In Australia, the Commonwealth Bank has outsourced its information technology, printing, record centres, supply functions and mail operations. In some of its mines, Western Mining Corporation owns the gold and nickel deposits, but the labour and management of the mining process has been outsourced (Long, 1998; Syvret, 1998).

Much has been written about the criteria that should guide decisions to outsource, and both successes and failures have been reported in the press. The financial press, in particular, tends to focus on the size of the contract, and the identity of the outsourcer who wins the bid. Outsourcing 'successes' and 'failures' are often judged by whether the firm achieves cost savings, or experiences cost overruns. Few reports, however, consider the importance of the relationship between the firm and the outsourcer, and the contribution that a co-operative relationship can make to a successful outsourcing partnership. A mismanaged relationship between a firm and its outsourcer may have serious implications for the firm's long-term strategy, continued competitiveness and profitability, even when the initial outsourcing decision was well conceived. On the other hand, a well managed relationship can be highly beneficial to both the firm and the outsourcer.

A major focus of this report is on answering two questions: What are the important issues that must be managed within an outsourcing relationship? Is it more difficult to control an outsourced activity, compared to an in-house activity? The decision processes and experiences of four Australian organisations that have outsourced major functions provide the background to addressing these questions.

What is outsourcing?

Outsourcing is the contracting of any service or activity to a third party organisation (McHugh, Merli and Wheeler, 1995; Drtina, 1994). It is often described as a form of 'vertical disintegration', and has been both praised and criticised (Eroglu, 1994; Walker and Weber, 1984). Outsourcing is increasingly being applied, not only to manufacturing activities, but to traditional in-house administrative and management functions, including data processing and information technology operations, human resource management services, accounting functions, internal audit and marketing (Chalos, 1995).

Outsourcing contracts may be of a significant size. For example, in 1993, British Telecom Australia (BTA) won a tender to manage the supply of voice and data networks and telecommunications services to the NSW Government (Plunkett, 1995). This ten-year contract was worth many hundreds of millions of dollars to BTA. Microsoft Australia outsourced its software support service to Wang Australia under a three-year contract worth around $3.3 million per year and, worldwide, Microsoft outsourced its software packaging and distribution (Banaghan, 1995). In the government sector up to 20 per cent of spending by the NSW Government relates to outsourced services that provide energy, transport and water services (Domberger and Farago, 1994). There is also widespread use of outsourcing by local councils across areas which include rubbish collection, road construction and the provision of welfare and community services (Rimmer, 1994).

Outsourcing may be undertaken to varying degrees. In many situations, the relationship between an organisation and an outsourcer resembles a partnership, rather than a traditional customer–supplier relationship (McHugh et al., 1995). In these partnerships, developing close co-operative relationships can be an important contributor to the success of the outsourcing venture (Langfield-Smith and Greenwood, 1998). In some situations, outsourcers are located on site, and capital equipment and staff may be transferred to the outsourcers. In other cases, equipment is owned jointly by the company and outsourcer. These issues add dimensions— beyond those applying in the traditional customer–supplier relationships—to the relationship between a company and an outsourcer.

What should be outsourced?

It is argued that, to achieve a long-term competitive advantage, a firm should focus on its core competencies, and outsource activities for which the firm has neither a critical strategic need, nor special capabilities (Quinn, 1992; Quinn and Hilmer, 1994; Hamel and Prahalad, 1994). As activities or functions within organisations become increasingly specialised, many managers consider that specialist outsourcing firms can undertake these functions more successfully—at a lower cost and higher quality. These functions include information technology, human resource management services and specialised manufacturing functions.

However, what is a core competency? A variety of meanings has been associated with the term:

- activities traditionally performed in-house;
- activities critical to business performance;
- activities creating current or potential competitive advantage; and
- activities that will drive future growth, innovation, or rejuvenation (Alexander and Young, 1996).

Clearly, this range of definitions makes it difficult to determine those activities that are, or have the potential to be, core competencies. However, Hamel and Prahalad (1994) present a framework for defining core competencies. They argue that enduring core competencies should be defined in terms of intellectual and knowledge-based service capabilities, rather than technologies, physical assets or products which can be copied or improved on by competitors (Quinn, 1992; Hamel and Prahalad, 1994). For example, core competencies may be identified in terms of skills in managing certain proprietary manufacturing processes, innovative research and development, marketing expertise or distribution networks. A firm's core competencies will often consist of several mutually reinforcing skills, which are linked to provide the firm with a superiority that competitors cannot achieve (Quinn, 1992). These competencies should be more enduring than the products currently produced, not diminish with use, and be the platform from which the firm may launch successful new products in the future (Hamel and Prahalad, 1994; Domberger, 1998).

However, Domberger (1998) suggests that searching for, and identifying, core competencies does not provide a sound methodology for deciding whether to outsource. Except in some technology-intensive industries, proprietary technical knowledge is not the central basis for obtaining market leadership. Therefore, fear of losing technical competencies through outsourcing may be relevant to only a few businesses. Domberger (1998) also claims that using core competencies as the basis for the outsourcing decision may not be a sound methodology, as it ignores potential efficiencies gained through outsourcing. A sounder basis on which to make an outsourcing decision is that of specialisation, and hence relative efficiency. This is not inconsistent with 'promoters' of the core competency argument. Quinn (1992), for example, argues that continuing to undertake activities that cannot be performed to 'world's best standard' will potentially reduce the firm's overall competitive edge.

Thus, it seems that basing the outsourcing decision on identifying core competencies is contentious. Not only is there some uncertainty as to what a core competency is, but, at least in some industries, it seems that such competencies may not be based on unique technology-based knowledge skills. Where this uniqueness is not relevant, outsourcing these aspects of the business may not pose a competitive threat for the firm and the outsourcing decision may be made with due consideration of cost efficiencies and specialisation.

However, outsourcing decisions involve more than just a consideration of core competencies or cost efficiencies. Important factors in any decision to outsource include a consideration of the strategic implications of the decision, identification of the expected benefits and limitations of outsourcing, and the impact on human resources within the organisation. The criteria that were used in four Australian organisations to guide their outsourcing decisions are explored within this study.

What are the benefits of outsourcing?

Outsourcing is said to lead to increased access to specialised skills, improved time-to-market, strengthening of core competencies, and cost savings. These benefits, in turn, may result in increased cost efficiencies, greater product quality and flexibility, and improvements in a firm's overall competitiveness.

Access to specialised skills

It is claimed that outsourcers provide wider access to specialist skills. The outsourcing provider may be at the leading edge of practice and technology in a specialised area, offering a level of expertise that a company cannot provide in-house. The emergence of rapidly changing specialist technologies has encouraged the development of specialist service companies which can leverage economies of scale and scope to provide high value-added services. In addition, full utilisation can be made of the outsourcer's investments, innovations and capabilities that would be prohibitively expensive to duplicate inside the firm.

Time-to-market

The outsourcing of product design or the manufacturing of key components may reduce design-time and time-to-market when several suppliers work in parallel on individual activities (Quinn, 1992). For companies operating in rapidly changing product markets, the time-to-market for a product is an essential aspect of competitive advantage.

Strengthening core competencies

Outsourcing allows firms to focus their resources and efforts on developing, or strengthening, their core competencies. This may provide a way to block competitors strategically, by creating permanence in selected areas which competitors would find difficult to overtake (Quinn and Hilmer, 1994). Outsourcing also creates advantages through the creation of strategic coalitions with the world's best suppliers.

Cost savings

When outsourcers are specialists in their own area of competence, they can deliver a product or service at a much lower cost compared to in-house delivery. Specialist outsourcing firms should be able to operate more cost effectively as they can build up economies of scale through their focus on their particular specialisation.

The downside of outsourcing

Against these benefits, the potential limitations of outsourcing must be considered. These include interrelated issues of the 'hollowing out' of the organisation, loss of skills and expertise, and loss of control over key processes and technologies.

'Hollowing out' of the organisation

A common criticism of outsourcing relates to the potential 'hollowing out' of the firm. When firms outsource major administrative and production functions, they greatly reduce in size. At the extreme, the organisation may become 'virtual' and comprise only a small group of in-house staff who manage a vast network of contractors. It is claimed that this leads to a loss of technological and human skills advantages associated with the functions that are outsourced, and leads to a loss of competitiveness (Eroglu, 1994). However, there is limited evidence to support this claim: in fact, many virtual organisations operate successfully. For example, Benetton outsources nearly all of its manufacturing and retail operations, and is considered highly successful (Lorenzoni and Baden-Fuller, 1995).

Loss of skills, knowledge and expertise

Decisions taken to outsource certain functions can be difficult to reverse where they involve a divestiture of both physical and human assets. For example, a common reason for companies' outsourcing information technology functions is the increasingly specialised nature of these services and the ongoing high capital investments required to maintain high value-added services in-house. However, the consequent loss of in-house expertise in that function may be difficult to re-establish if outsourcing is found to be a poor decision. A careful consideration of what constitutes the source of a company's competitive advantage and the choice of which functions to outsource 'safely' are critical.

Loss of control

A common criticism of outsourcing is that it may lead to a loss of control over critical organisational functions and knowledge. Outsourcing involves a sharing of information and technologies, so there is potential for an outsourcing decision to result in a supplier gaining competitive strength, and even setting up as a competitor.

While many companies consider that only activities that are not critical to the firm's strategy should be outsourced, it has been suggested that activities that are integral to a strategy may also be outsourced, provided sufficient controls and monitoring are introduced (Quinn, 1992; Lacity, Willcocks, and Feeny, 1995).

Managing the outsourcing relationship

The success or failure of an outsourcing activity is not dependent only on the criteria used to make the outsourcing decision. Processes and systems are needed to manage the new organisational relationship and control the outsourced operations. Limited research has been undertaken to identify the management issues relevant to outsourcing relationships. Nevertheless, it is likely that important mechanisms include the contract, communication channels, performance monitoring and the use of informal controls.

The contract

As most outsourcing arrangements span several years and involve large sums of money, there is usually a formal contract between the firm and the outsourcer. The contract provides the opportunity for the two parties to agree on how a range of issues will be managed before the work passes to the outsourcer. Typically, the contract specifies the obligations that each party has to the other, performance indicators and financial arrangements, procedures to be undertaken in the event of a dispute, and provisions for termination.

Contracts allow both parties to consider the nature of the relationship in the new undertaking, and specify the ground rules at the start of the relationship. However, it is difficult to include all of the important aspects within a contract, as it becomes too cumbersome and inflexible. In addition, it is difficult to foresee all contingencies that may arise over the course of the relationship and include them within the formal agreement. Therefore, the contract is only the starting point in setting up systems to manage the outsourcing relationship.

Communication channels

An important aspect of effective relationship management is the establishment of a 'protocol' for communication between the parties. While relationships need to develop between the outsourcer and the 'customers' at all levels within the firm, to avoid confusion there needs to initially be a single point of contact between the firm and the outsourcer (Bendor-Samuel, 1999). This contact person should be highly skilled in the area being outsourced. For example, for information technology outsourcing, the contact person should be a highly skilled IT professional. In addition, strong relationships need to develop between the senior managements of the outsourcer and the firm to make it easier to solve conflicts when they arise.

Performance monitoring

It has been suggested that a firm may gain control over the function being outsourced through ongoing monitoring of the work performance, as well as monitoring aspects of the outsourcing relationship throughout the contract period (McFarlan and Nolan, 1995). This may be achieved through the use of performance measures and benchmarks which focus on areas such as customer satisfaction, delivery responsiveness, product quality and cost. These may be included in the contract, or may be negotiated at a later time.

Informal controls

Whether we are referring to controls within a single firm, or between a firm and an outsourcer, the implementation of formal control systems may not be sufficient to achieve effective control. It may be necessary to also rely on informal mechanisms, the existence of which is highly dependent on the nature of the relationships that build up between the parties. For example, the development of a greater degree of information sharing can assist in operating decisions. High levels of trust, although difficult to achieve, may also help a firm facilitate effective control.

Is control different under outsourcing?

An important question to address when considering how to manage an outsourcer relationship is whether the management issues are different for outsourced functions, as compared to in-house functions. Are there different control issues that emerge when firms rely on outsourcers? Are there unique management problems that arise when functions are outsourced? As there is limited research addressing these questions, they are explored in later chapters.

The most obvious issue that should lead to a difference between in-house and outsourced functions arises from the legal separation that exists between the firm and the outsourcer. Grabner (1993) uses the term 'embedded firms' to describe the situation where steps within the production of goods or services take place in legally separate organisations. Thus, when an outsourcer is contracted, various activities within the value chain are undertaken inside and outside the organisation. What forms of control are possible in embedded firms?

There are two primary sources of formal control within firms; direct control (through direct supervision and oversight of staff) and indirect control (through delegation of responsibilities, and reporting and performance monitoring systems). In an embedded organisation, direct supervision of activities performed by the outsourcer's employees is usually not appropriate, as the outsourcer is an autonomous legal entity. Also, it cannot be assumed that a firm has direct and immediate access to information held by the outsourcer. Indirect controls such as performance measures may be used, and these may be included in outsourcing contracts. However, the degree of authority of a manager over an outsourcer may be quite different to that over employees. It is less likely that new systems for control can be imposed on an outsourcer without a fair degree of negotiation, and such systems may simply be rejected. Also, co-ordination and monitoring may be difficult if the outsourcer is an expert in a field in which the firm has little expertise.

Another barrier to control over an outsourcer relates to differences in the cultures of a firm and its outsourcer, such as different values, strategies, goals and ways of operating. Within a firm, shared cultural values are an important source of control. However, different values in the two organisations may create difficulties in developing and managing the relationship, lead to misunderstandings and mistrust, and force a greater reliance on formal controls.

The focus of this study

Many of the recent case studies on outsourcing examine the outsourcing of data processing and information systems (see for example Lacity and Hirschheim, 1993; McFarlan and Nolan, 1995). However, outside of these areas, there are few case studies that investigate the motivation underlying the decision to outsource, the ongoing management of the outsourcing contract, and the control issues that may be associated with managing an outsourced operation. In this study, a variety of outsourced functions is considered, and the management and control issues form a particular focus. The four organisations that participated in the study operate in very different industries and environments, and the functions that they outsourced vary. Table 1 summarises the characteristics of each firm. Data were collected through interviews with managers and the inspection of company documents.

Within each of the four firms, the following issues were considered:

- What motivated the firm to consider outsourcing?
- What criteria were used to evaluate the outsourcing decision?
- What issues were important in managing the outsourcing relationship?
- What were the benefits gained from outsourcing?
- What lessons emerged from the outsourcing experience?

This leads to a consideration of the following two questions:

- What are the important issues that must be managed within an outsourcing relationship?
- Is it more difficult to control an outsourced activity, compared to an in-house activity?

The experiences of the four firms are discussed in the following four chapters. The concluding chapter identifies the common and unique issues that emerged from the study, and draws some conclusions.

Table 1
Organisations in the study

Organisation[1]	Industry	Main activities outsourced
Gradient Steel	Steel manufacturer	Collection of scrap for reprocessing Removal of slag Maintenance of cast mouldings
Central Energy	Electricity and gas provider	Information technology services
Greentrees Council	Local council	Road and bridge construction and maintenance Parks maintenance Aquatic centre management Childcare centres
ElectNet	Manager of electricity network	Information technology services

[1] The name of each organisation has been changed to preserve anonymity.

2

GRADIENT STEEL

Background

Gradient Steel (Gradient) is a manufacturing site within a large steel company. Throughout the 1990s, the company was under increasing pressure from the financial market to develop a new strategic direction and to improve its financial performance. Several divisions within the larger company downsized and underwent restructuring, and many senior managers were replaced as the company tried to turn its fortunes around and regain the confidence of the financial market. At the start of 1997, Gradient employed about 1100 people. The main manufacturing functions included ironmaking, slabmaking, rolling mills and coating facilities. The plant produced around 4.8 million tonnes of steel per annum.

Types of outsourcing activities

Gradient began outsourcing activities in the late 1980s. The emphasis was on keeping the core activities of the business in-house, whilst outsourcing activities for which the business had neither a critical strategic need nor special capabilities.

By 1997, 40 per cent of the people working on-site at Gradient were employed by outsourcers. The outsourcers provided major services (such as scrap processing) and minor services (such as plant maintenance). Major outsourcers, many of which were located permanently on-site, conducted activities that were essential to the steel-making operations. In contrast, providers of minor services only came on-site to provide their particular service.

Major services

By 1997, Gradient had outsourced major operations to 25 different companies who operated on land leased to them by the company. These companies brought technology, capital equipment or expenditure, and people as part of the outsourcing arrangement. They became an integral part of the operations of Gradient and over time, the relationship between the company and the outsourcers became more of a partnership than the traditional customer–supplier relationship. The operations undertaken by three of these organisations (Bunbury, Mercury and Artio) are described below.

Bunbury, a maintenance contractor, had special expertise in maintaining cast moulds and brought in plant and equipment as part of the agreement. The contractor also employed Gradient's maintenance staff, who were made redundant following the commencement of the outsourcing contract.

Mercury provided 20 per cent of the feed to the steel-making shop. It collected scrap from around Gradient's site and transported it to a centralised collection area. The scrap was sorted and, after the removal of dangerous material, packaged into the correct 'mix', loaded into skips and transported to the steel-making shop where it was used in the furnace. Gradient estimated that the set-up costs for Mercury were $15 million.

Artio collected and moved molten slag to one location for processing and stockpiling. Two main types of slag were produced: ironmaking slag (from the blast furnace) which was turned into a product used in the cement industry, and steel-making slag which was predominantly used as a substitute for quarry rock in road construction. It was estimated by managers at Gradient that Artio invested $30 million to set up its operation on the site.

Minor services

A large number of outsourcers performed services that were considered peripheral to Gradient's operations. These included the contracting of minor services for the metal facing and engineering division; the provision of electrical, fitting, and boilermaking services; the management of canteens; and the cleaning of windows and offices.

In the maintenance area, Gradient used both in-house people and outsourcers. In the mid-1990s, the company moved away from hiring a range of contractors for 'one-off jobs' on an hourly or a lump sum basis to three-year contracts with fewer contractors. An engineering contracts manager explained the rationale behind the change:

> To get the best performance, the manufacturing process needs to flow, and it is very sensitive to interruptions. So, it's most important that we get very good maintenance. By letting the maintenance company win that work, it has security, it has better access to bank loans, and it can give us a cheaper price so we win both ways.

Motivation for outsourcing

Reasons for engaging in outsourcing at Gradient included:

- the desire to achieve increased workforce flexibility;
- access to specialised skills and technology; and
- the need for improved cost effectiveness.

Flexibility of wages and conditions

In the late 1980s, Gradient's workforce was employed under rigid award conditions. This was one of the initial reasons for outsourcing non-core activities to contractors whose employees were cheaper, multi-skilled and prepared to work more flexible hours. However, in the 1990s many changes took place in the industrial relations environment, and the wages and flexibility of Gradient's employees and the outsourcer's employees moved closer together.

As Gradient moved to outsource services to a smaller number of larger contractors, the union began to work with employees of the outsourcers to bring their conditions in line with those of employees of Gradient. At the same time, Gradient's employees adopted more flexible work practices and became more multi-skilled. As stated by an engineering contracts manager, the workforce became '… more targeted towards the performance of what it does, rather than just working another hour for x dollars.' Thus, over time, the advantage of flexibility of wages and conditions offered by an outsourcer was eroded and ceased to be a compelling reason for outsourcing.

Access to expertise and technology

Opportunities to use specialised expertise and gain access to the latest technology provided reasons for Gradient's outsourcing of certain functions. For example, Bunbury had special expertise in maintaining cast moulds,

Mercury proposed the remote loading of skips to overcome Gradient's scrap handling problems, and Artio had expertise in marketing slag. A business planning manager explained the approach:

> You need to convince yourself that this other party has some expertise that exceeds your own, that it is more their core business, rather than your core business and therefore they can succeed better at it than you can.

Cost effectiveness

Steel production is a cyclical business which, in the early 1990s, went through a particularly depressed time. The decision to outsource was also driven by the need to be more cost-effective. Pressures from the parent company reinforced the need to improve cost effectiveness and profitability.

Criteria used in the outsourcing decision

A number of criteria were used by Gradient to decide whether to outsource an activity. These included:

- whether the function was a core or non-core activity;
- the availability of specialised service providers;
- clear financial benefits to Gradient;
- attention of the outsourcer to safety and environmental issues; and
- human resource management issues.

Core or non-core activities

As a general policy, Gradient was only willing to outsource activities that it believed were not core to its business. However, as with many businesses, managers at the company found it difficult to distinguish between core and non-core activities. A manager of business planning provided an example of the debate:

> We have a live project that revolves around ejecting powdered coal into the blast furnace. There are a number of companies that do this for steel makers in other parts of the world and they're experts at pulverising coal and conveying it pneumatically via downpipes and into the blast furnace—but they don't know anything about running blast furnaces ... The debate we're having at the moment is whether it is sufficiently non-core for us to allow a third party to do it, because they could influence the smooth running of the blast furnaces if they don't do it well.

Before a function was considered a possible candidate for outsourcing, a decision was made as to whether the service was vital to the manufacturing process from a technical perspective, and whether it was unique to the steel-making process. An engineering service manager explained the risk associated with losing technical expertise:

> We would start to lose our currency in that technology and we would be exposed to the outsourcer suddenly deciding that they would like to go somewhere else themselves.

An interesting example of an outsourcing decision related to scrap. Many managers believed that scrap reprocessing was close to the core business. This was something that had always been managed in-house, as it was a critical part of the production process (incorrectly processed scrap could be a safety hazard). A manager explained the dilemma:

> In those days, our scrap handling was so diverse. We were handling scrap on six different locations around the steel works with all sorts of equipment. We had at least five different contractors involved in some parts of the scrap handling so it was a real muddle and so we called for tenders from interested parties to see how they would propose to handle our scrap. That is when Mercury came up with the winning entry. Part of the motivation for the move to outsource was that some of our people had taken a study tour to see how the rest of the world were handling scrap, and they saw many examples where a contractor from another company was providing the service. The proposal that Mercury presented was very different to the way we would do it, particularly with the remote loading of skips, which was always considered to be something you did inside the steel-making shop. The concept of carting them around the site was a little foreign to us.

Thus, Gradient clearly considered that it was not an expert in the handling of scrap and, whether or not it was a core activity, it was clearly more efficient and cost-effective to engage a specialist outsourcer.

The availability of service providers

Another guideline was whether there was a range of companies who had the capacity to provide that particular service. An engineering service manager explained:

> If there is only one company that has the capacity for technical or resource reasons, you'd think carefully whether you want to expose yourself to that or not.

The risk associated with placing too much reliance on a single specialised service provider was an issue that Gradient considered carefully. It did not want to be tied exclusively to a single provider, or to face the possibility of dependence.

Financial benefits

Outsourcing proposals for major services were subject to the same capital authorisation procedures as capital expenditure requests for assets or other projects.

A proposal was provided to the business planning department, which evaluated the project to determine whether it made 'good business sense' and then considered possible sources of finance. Business planning also prepared the formal submission using checklists. Where appropriate, advice was sought from experts on legal, tax and human resource issues. Projects valued less than $10 million were authorised by the CEO of the Steel Division, and greater than $10 million required Board authorisation.

To outsource an activity, a clear economic benefit to the business needed to be demonstrated. In Gradient, it was found that the benefits from outsourcing projects tended to be overestimated, often due to the enthusiasm of the manager proposing the project. Consequently, a high hurdle rate was used to help ensure that clear benefits would result from any outsourcing contract that was implemented.

It was important to demonstrate that the outsourcing decision would have a clear benefit to the business, rather than being viewed as an easy opportunity to gain access to additional equipment. A business planning manager explained the internal pressures for outsourcing:

> One of the things you will find in an organisation like this is that it is very capital intensive, and we are very strong on engineering. We have a lot of people who are builders and operators and there's always demand for capital which can't be justified in terms of returns ... so people look to outsourcing proposals as an opportunity to avoid the capital budget. So part of my finance role is to make sure that people look at outsourcing contracts for the right reasons ... If the reason is to restrict capital investment, then that's the wrong reason.

As for all capital expenditure proposals at Gradient, a Capital Expenditure Checklist was prepared for each outsourcing proposal. Examples of information included were assumptions about risk exposures, tariffs, technology, taxation, expected life of the project, sensitivity analysis on financial indicators to account for variations in key assumptions, prior costs (for example, feasibility study costs, engineering, market research), key performance indicators, and time frame (ten–twenty years depending on the service). Marketing information included market size, current market selling prices, relative market share, volumes, and competitor reactions.

Managing the interface between Gradient and the outsourcers was recognised as potentially significant, so transaction costs were included in the evaluation process. A manager of business planning described how this has changed over the years:

> If you looked at the analyses we've done of the contracts going back a few years you would be hard-pressed to find some recognition of transaction costs. However, now we have had a lot of experience with outsourcing. The analyses we do now are more searching in terms of financial evaluation than they were three–five years ago.

The cost of the time involved in managing the outsourcing contracts needed to be estimated because transaction cost information was not captured in the company's costing systems.

Safety and environmental issues

Gradient was responsible for all people on its site, including employees, visitors, and outsourcers' employees. Thus, increased emphasis came to be placed on evaluating the safety practices and environmental values of potential outsourcers. The cost to Gradient of training the outsourcers' employees in occupational health and safety and environmental issues was also included in the initial evaluation process. A process and service contracts manager explained the approach:

> We try to assess what the company's track record has been, we access information from around the nation and around the world: How do they value safety? How do they value the environment? These are becoming much more important considerations in our outsourcing decisions.

Human resource management issues

In evaluating the impact of outsourcing on employees, Gradient investigated a range of aspects, including the approaches to industrial relations and voluntary retrenchment payments. A process and service manager explained the problem when an outsourcing company had a different industrial relations approach to that of the company:

> If the company we outsource to has a completely different IR approach, and they are positioned on our property, then it is damn difficult for our workforce. The industrial relations ramifications were not originally built into the outsourcing decision-making process, and to that extent we slipped up. We managed to get over it, but it took a large amount of resources. In addition, we ended up restructuring our contracts anyhow.

In some cases, the new outsourcer might offer employment to Gradient's employees when an internal function was discontinued in favour of an outsourcer. One manager explained:

Our displaced employees were given offers of employment by Bunbury. Whenever we're doing something that could be seen as our employees' giving up their jobs in favour of other things, we do a great deal to try and manage the industrial relations side of things. With the major ones, we have worked with local union officials to make that outcome come about. We usually try to have a win–win situation for the employees and us.

Managing the outsourcing relationship

As mentioned previously, Gradient's experience with outsourcing commenced in the late 1980s. Since that time, it has developed several mechanisms to help manage relationships with outsourcers. These include the following:

- the use of key performance indicators and performance measures;
- monitoring of occupational health and safety and the environment;
- co-ordinating production;
- determining responsibility for costs; and
- post-implementation reviews.

Key performance indicators

An important aspect of evaluating the performance of the outsourcer, and managing the relationship between the two parties, is the use of key performance indicators (KPIs). Gradient created a large infrastructure to manage the growing number of outsourcing contracts. As well as a Contracts Management Steering Committee, there were a number of subcommittees. Regular reviews were conducted, based on performance against the KPIs contained within the contract, and on other issues that arose during the month. The KPIs were managed between the contractor and the customer departments, with the supply department playing a co-ordinating role. A business planning manager explained how the company defined KPIs:

KPIs are few in number. They are very focused and you cannot enjoy success without achieving the KPIs. So if the business or its operation seems to be running to your complete satisfaction yet it is not achieving KPIs, then it wasn't a true KPI in the first place ... It's got to be key to being able to satisfy your business requirements.

Another issue in developing KPIs was controllability. That is, it was important to ensure that the outsourcer could control the KPI it was being measured against. A process and service contracts manager explained:

One of the fundamentals of KPIs at Gradient is that they have to measure an outcome that a particular service provider or internal person in the company is able to have a major influence over. For example, 'tonnes of slag' is not a KPI, as the outsourcer has no control over how much slag is produced.

Over time a number of outsourcing contracts were restructured to focus on only a few 'all-encompassing' KPIs. A process and service contracts manager explained:

> Another lesson that we are learning with outsourcing is to develop the real key, fundamental KPIs. In my experience there are only two or three KPIs for each operation. The rest are performance indicators or just monitors.

KPIs played an important role in managing the interface between Gradient and the outsourcers. For example, Artio, which was involved in the removal and stockpiling of molten slag, served three internal customers, and three sets of KPIs were developed to ensure that the needs of each customer were addressed, as well as providing incentives for the outsourcer. For the transport and site services, three KPIs were based on revenue and stock levels; whilst, for the steel and iron makers, KPIs related to the removal of slag without interrupting production processes. A process and service contracts manager explained how KPIs were used in the Artio contract to help manage the complex relationship:

> When you are outsourcing a service which serves many internal customer groups, who are all very big and important and fairly autonomous, one of the things that is very important is that we get our act together and make sure that the left and right hand know what is key, and what are going to be the measures of success, and that particular arrangement has been somewhat disappointing to us.

Similarly, a manager of business planning explained that KPIs could aid in reducing the cost of managing the interface between Gradient and the outsourcing contractors:

> When we are making an outsourcing decision, one of the advantages is that it allows our management to focus on what it does best. But there is the downside of having to manage the contract. That is where you can be clever at setting up a contract in the first place, with KPIs that give the other party some incentive to improve, and which minimise our ongoing cost of managing the contract.

There was a growing recognition of the need to continuously manage the outsourcing of major services, which were closely integrated into Gradient's operations. At the time of writing this case, the company was developing a customer satisfaction process to review long-term outsourcing contracts every two or three years as a basis for identifying changes and improvements that should be made. This would involve the following processes:

> The key internal customers will reassess what is important to them, rank order

those, and then assess, jointly with the outsourcer, how they are performing against those to date. If there are two or more areas of our operation involved, we need to go through that process even more rigorously, and get the right weightings on what is important. Most of these companies we outsource to are small relative to us, and I have seen them get totally confused with what it is that we want. So we will size up their current service delivery to constructively identify gaps and then consider how we close those gaps: Is it actioned by them? Is it actioned by us? Or jointly actioned? We are finding the need to use this type of rigorous process becomes even more important if it is a larger arrangement and if there are multiple internal customers.

Gradient was also encouraging outsourcers to introduce KPIs to assess their internal customers within the company. This was not successful, however, because the outsourcers generally did not want to criticise 'the hand that feeds them'. A process and services manager gave the following example of trying to improve the system of payments to outsourcers:

We were not very good at paying them on time and this kept on coming up. We put the performance indicator together, and our performance was awful. There is now a small project team involving the outsourcer's people and our own to improve that, but it is still not on the official agenda. We're only just starting but I am sure that over the five–ten years we'll see a significant movement down that track because there's no doubt that there is a lot of improvement that we need to make. This can only come about if it's not done on an adversarial or contractual basis—both parties need to recognise that a certain problem exists and then work together to solve it.

Occupational health, safety and the environment

Gradient was responsible for the environment, health and safety issues of all the people who came on-site under the occupational health and safety and environmental protection legislation. A process and service contracts manager explained how they were spending more time on these issues:

We accept our responsibility as owners of property and on that basis we have to be satisfied that everything that is happening on our property is in line with what the legislation requires, and what we require. It is not enough any more simply to say, 'well, that's their problem', because it's ours as well as theirs.

This responsibility was especially difficult for Gradient as, by 1997, approximately 40 per cent of the workforce on-site were working for outsourced contractors. A manager of business planning explained:

We have to make best endeavours to ensure their safety, their welfare and their health. Now that can get a little hard to do with people who are not directly working for you. The environment situation is probably tougher than health and safety. The EPA has been very specific on this. If we get another party to handle some of our noxious activities like dipping slag, that gives rise to pollution, they're very keen that we don't try and off-load our responsibility onto someone else. They do not want to chase Mercury and Artio; they will chase us. So yes, we require outcomes that meet the same high standards of safety and environmental management.

The Mercury contract was a good example of how outsourcing increased the complexity of health, safety and environmental matters for Gradient because this was the first time the company had put its safety and quality control into the hands of outsourcers. A manager of business planning explained:

> You have to be very careful with scrap because it explodes ... there are some nasties that can get into the scrap which, if you don't have a good quality control system, would create havoc for the steel-making operation.

Recognising the importance of building relationships, Gradient invited the outsourcers' employees to participate in safety programs alongside company employees. A process and service contracts manager explained:

> Now we have a two-day job safety management program which has been running for about 120 of our front-line supervisors. The contractors have worked closely with us. They have all been given the opportunity to participate in that and we want them to train their own trainers, to train their own people. But we do not want their people and our people at loggerheads about process and what is required. Therefore, we work very closely with the companies that we outsource to, to establish common understandings about these issues.

Over time, outsourcers became integrated into the quality management systems, and spent considerable time training the workforce to understand its safety, quality, and delivery requirements.

Co-ordinating production

Another issue that was difficult to manage was the time spent in managing the production interface between Gradient and the outsourcers. The major outsourced activities were critical to the smooth operation of the plant. For example, Artio was operating equipment that handled the liquid slag as it left the furnace and production problems resulted if the equipment was not at the furnace at the right time. Similarly, Mercury supplied approximately 20 per cent of the feed for the steel-making shop. There were severe disruptions if the scrap mixture was not of the right quality, or their skips did not arrive on time.

Responsibility for costs

One issue that was difficult to manage was determining who had the responsibility for the cost of replacing equipment. Many of the outsourcers were located on-site, and in some cases they were sharing facilities with Gradient. A senior manager provided an example of one issue that arose with an outsourcer:

> It is not a major occupier of time but there have been one or two cases where we have had a great deal of difficulty agreeing who should pay for something. The scrap skips are large and quite expensive to maintain. Mercury uses skips to move scrap to the furnace, but we also use them to scrape material off the furnace, and that of course causes damage to the scrap skips. Our contract with Mercury says they maintain the scrap skips, but if the scrap skip is damaged due to our mistreatment, we say, 'We've always performed that operation this way. You knew that when you entered this contract' and they say, 'Oh we didn't know that you were going to drop it'. We might have dropped it but that's just part of the operation, and they say that's negligence. So you can get into a bit of a bind as to who is going to pay for the thing.

A difficult issue here is how specific written agreements need to be, if they are to account for contingencies such as this.

Post-implementation review

A post-implementation review of all outsourcing contracts was required twelve months after commencement. This included a review of the original proposal, details of cost overruns, performance to KPIs and performance indicators and any strategic implications of the contract. This was the same form of review used for all capital expenditure projects. A senior financial manager explained the purpose of the review:

> The main focus of a post-implementation review is lessons learnt, to build up an information base. Although we want to report back on how much we have spent and what were the benefits of the project, the financials are not the main purpose for doing a post-implementation review. It is important to report if something went wrong in managing HR issues or industrial relations issues on a project. On average, we fall short of our expectations on major projects, and this is a problem. We tend to be starry-eyed as to what the project is going to bring in. It is usually sobering. You learn a lot about lowering your expectations, but also the reasons why you failed. Some of the main reasons that re-occur are our inability to correctly read the forward markets for the price, and the marketability of what we are doing. Over-expenditure of capital is another big one.

Benefits of outsourcing

There were a number of benefits for Gradient that arose from the outsourcing of major services. These included:

- access to specialised expertise;
- improved plant efficiencies; and
- financial benefits.

Access to expertise

Outsourcing of major services gave Gradient access to outsourcers who had developed expertise in specialised areas. The Bunbury contract, for example, provided special expertise in maintaining cast moulds. Another benefit was an increase in the number of heats per day, which was a key performance factor for the plant.

Plant efficiencies

Several of the outsourcers implemented new systems and procedures which resulted in quality improvements and more efficient operations. For example, the rationalisation of facilities was one of the key advantages arising from the Mercury contract. This affected health, safety and environment through the use of fume extraction equipment on-site, and truck movements reduced by one-tenth. In addition, Mercury developed a higher level of quality control on-site, and cost savings flowed on to Gradient.

Financial benefits

Many of the major outsourcing contracts generated direct financial benefits for Gradient. For example, as part of one contract, the company earned royalties from the sales of slag made by Artio, instead of having to pay a fee to dispose of slag. Gradient had previously been unsuccessful in marketing the slag themselves. Outsourcing of minor services also provided a number of advantages for Gradient. For example, using experts in industrial cleaning to clean the BOS vessel (which made steel from iron) saved $800 000 per annum in direct costs and increased the availability of the vessel for steel-making by 90 hours per annum.

In many situations it was difficult to determine the precise cost savings that resulted from an outsourcing activity, as many of the costs cut across several cost centres and the costing system was not flexible enough to track through the costs associated with a particular activity.

Lessons learned

Gradient began outsourcing in the late 1980s, and over this time learned a number of key lessons about improving the initial evaluation of the outsourcing contract, and managing the outsourcing relationship.

Improving the initial evaluation process

Gradient learned to improve the initial evaluation process for outsourcing proposals. Post-implementation reviews indicated that the financial evaluations tended to be over optimistic. Some of the main problems were the inability to correctly estimate the forward markets for the price and marketability of the product, and over-expenditure of capital. The emphasis changed towards carrying out more detailed evaluations to ensure there was a clear benefit from outsourcing. For example, the financial evaluation changed to include transaction costs and training costs (to ensure compliance with safety and environment needs). In addition to the financial evaluation, there came to be a greater emphasis on evaluating the values and business practices of the outsourcer (such as in the areas of industrial relations and safety) because the outsourcers were integral to Gradient's operations.

A process and service contracts manager explained how important it was in future contracts to evaluate the safety practices of any potential outsourcer:

> It would be fair to say that, in the past, most of the issues about safety and the environment have been dealt with after we entered into an outsourcing contract. However, in any new outsourcing arrangements, about 80 per cent of the safety and environmental management would be done before we even signed the contract.

While this chapter has focused on the major services that Gradient outsourced, there was also an increased level of outsourcing of minor services. This required the company to document the procedures for outsourcing maintenance contracts and ensuring quality control. The emphasis in the evaluation process moved away from identifying inputs, to specifying the performance requirements (that is, outputs) required by the internal customers (within Gradient). In addition, the focus moved towards establishing the criteria by which tenders would be judged, and then weighting each criterion by its relative importance to reduce bias in the decision making process.

Flexible contracts

The inflexibility of the outsourcing contracts was a major problem for Gradient. The company was under considerable pressure to reduce costs in the middle and late 1990s, but was unable to increase efficiency or save costs from the outsourcing contractors who were locked into long-term (fixed price) contracts. In addition, Gradient was committed to fixed volumes of service with outsourcers, which did not take into account process improvements that led to reductions in volume.

Consequently, Gradient re-negotiated some long-term contracts to build in flexibility, and to ensure that it received benefits from improvements as they occurred. A process and service contracts manager explained:

> The second time around, it becomes more important to build in the flexibility for us to take advantage of improvements, fairly shortly after they have been made, not five or ten or fifteen years later. These are improvements made by the contractor and/or improvements that build up between the contractor and us. It does tend to reduce the risk profile to the contractor because we want to participate in benefits sooner rather than later.

Re-negotiation of a contract

When re-negotiating a contract, several additional considerations were often taken into account. A process and services manager provided this example of the evaluation process used when deciding whether to continue an outsourcing contract for major services:

> We had a seven-year outsourcing arrangement and we re-evaluated whether or not we would continue to outsource that particular service, do it ourselves on-site, or just have it provided off-site. In comparison to seven years ago when the original decision was made, more emphasis was given to evaluating the impact of the continuing contract on the security of our property. Some outsourcing contracts can involve other companies processing gases, liquids and solids on-site, and this has implications for security. This contract was one of those. Another consideration was that a lot of the investment associated with that outsourced service had effectively been paid for through the service fee, and the area that we had leased to that company needed only minimal reinvestment to keep it going. Relocating the service off-site would entail a significant cost, because it involved movement of heavy equipment. So we worked through the issues: What's the relocation cost? What is the cost to keep it running on this site? What are the entry costs for another company to come in and provide the service? It was pretty obvious that the best thing to do was to keep it on-site but we were unhappy about what we were paying for the service, so the contractor was asked to put forward a new proposal. Ironically, we have been pursuing a 20 per cent cost reduction program inside our company, and when we netted out the extra capital on everything they had built into their offer, it also represented a 20 per cent reduction. In more recent times, we have not been entirely happy with some outsourcing arrangements, because we put a lot of pressure on our own people to improve cost performance, and while the contractors are clearly improving, the benefits do not always flow through to us.

Clarifying relationships with internal customers

Gradient had some difficulties in managing complexity when some outsourcers had multiple internal customers. In these situations, KPIs helped by ensuring that people were focusing on the important issues. The systems changed from using many KPIs, toward focusing on simply the two or three KPIs that would ensure success of the service, and which could be influenced by the outsourcer.

Another lesson Gradient learned was to reduce the complexity of the relationships. For example, the company had an outsourcing agreement with two other companies to develop new technologies. However, the complexity of the arrangement made it difficult to assign responsibility for problems that were arising. This contract was restructured to include only one other company and, by focusing more on KPIs, performance improved.

3

CENTRAL ENERGY

Background

Central Energy (Central) was formed in 1995, through the merger of two electricity authorities, Hilton Energy (Hilton) and Woodside Electricity (Woodside). Central distributes and retails electricity and value-added energy services to more than one million people across a large diverse area. Central also sells major electrical contracting services throughout Australia and retails energy services to major industrial and commercial clients throughout New South Wales and Victoria.

Deregulation of the Australian electricity industry has led to considerable changes for organisations like Central. Increased competition has occurred through the privatisation or corporatisation of state-owned monopolies. In New South Wales, the industry has been broken up into a number of separate corporatised entities that manage electricity distribution, generation, and the electricity grid. Adding to the increased competitive pressure is the fact that since 1 January 2000, all customers have been able to buy their power from any of the state's electricity distributors. Thus, distributors can seek customers from other states, therefore making protection of the customer base even more difficult. Improved customer service and reduced costs have become prime considerations.

To remain competitive in this environment, Central established four separate businesses and a holding company. Each business is required to make a profit. When services are provided from one business to another, they are supplied on a commercial arms-length basis.

The outsourcing decision

At the time of the merger of the two electricity authorities, the executive steering committee made two strategic decisions. The first decision was to consider outsourcing the information technology function. The second decision was to review supply chain opportunities. This chapter focuses primarily on the outsourcing of the information technology and telecommunications (IT&T) function, which occurred within two months of the merger. Major supply chain decisions were made within the next eighteen months, and these new strategic alliances benefited from the firm's experiences of outsourcing IT&T.

Motivation for outsourcing IT&T

Central's written policy is to '… ensure that all internal services are provided effectively and efficiently to the core Network and Energy Services businesses'. Where this could not be achieved to a standard and at a cost available from external suppliers, competitive tenders were sought and evaluated. Where there was a clear economic and service standard advantage to Central, outsourcing was pursued.

It is clear from the above that cost effectiveness and strategic issues are primary considerations in outsourcing decisions made by Central. However, the specific factors that motivated the decision to outsource IT&T were broader and included:

- the search for a solution to the problem of merging two very different IT cultures;
- the need to improve cost management of IT&T;
- greater access to technical knowledge and expertise; and
- the need to bring more discipline and control to the IT&T function.

Merging of two IT cultures

The merger of the two electricity authorities brought together two IT&T functions that were very different in size and nature, as well as focus and direction. Developing a single, effective IT&T function was seen as a major managerial issue and an important determinant of the ability of Central to compete in the new contestable electricity environment. Hilton had 168 IT&T staff, compared with Woodside's 33 staff. Hilton was a mainframe environment with large-scale applications, and frequent cost overruns. Woodside had a very low cost infrastructure: its systems were small, not run on mainframes, and there were limited funds for software development. Many of Woodside's IT staff took voluntary redundancies with the merger.

Cost management

Before the merger there was poor cost management of the IT&T function, particularly on the Hilton side. Cost overruns were common, and there was little control over the initiation of new projects. Hilton's IT&T was strongly customer focused so that a plethora of operating systems was supported and new applications were continually under development. There was limited accountability for spending on IT resources. A senior manager described the situation:

> A business would ask IT&T for something to be done, but they were not being charged the true cost. There was no discipline in the management of costs. One of the drivers in relation to the move to outsource the IT&T area was to introduce that discipline, so that if you do ask for something to be modified or changed, someone comes back to you and says 'You know it's going to cost you $20 000 to do this'.

The transfer pricing system used to charge users of IT&T services 'sent the wrong signals', and led to dysfunctional decision making. Favours and 'funny prices' led to a lack of accountability and an absence of commercial reality. It was envisaged that outsourcing the IT&T function would help to curb spending, as money would be seen to be leaving the organisation, as opposed to the situation under the old transfer pricing system. An IT manager described past practices.

> The IT cost was like a bottomless bucket. The projects were actually controlled by the IT people, not by the users. They might have been initiated by the users, but basically the users lost control. So the IT people started to dominate the situation. Now that is the fault of the users, not a fault of the IT people. The organisation recognised that it did not manage that well.

While managers had some difficulty assessing the cost of in-house IT&T for the two electricity distributors before the merger, it was estimated at $42 million per year. Many managers, however, believed that this was overstated —the accounting systems were thought to be inaccurate. Nevertheless, IT&T was clearly a significant cost to the business and so provided opportunities for cost improvements.

Access to technical knowledge and expertise

Within Central, IT&T was not considered a core competency of the business, and it was clear that in the future the organisation would need to gain access to high levels of expertise. It was considered difficult and impractical to supply this in-house. One manager described the thinking:

> I think that at the end of the day, you really have to understand what are your core competencies. That is, what are the things that you are good at, that you do have an edge on and you really know the ins and outs of it. No matter what business you are in, there are some things that you can do better than others. It is a matter of identifying and really understanding those things. If you go back a few years, we probably did not really have a feel for that—we continued to do things because we had always done them. It is a matter of sitting down and saying, What are we good at? What can we compete with? With what things are we adding value to the organisation? And if there is some lineball exercise or some clear-cut situation where we are not adding value, then we have to think seriously about doing something else.

Central understood that its core business was energy services. The environment in which it was operating placed greater demands on the business for 'smarter systems', which would involve high use of sophisticated information technology. Thus, there would be greater reliance on the IT&T function in the future, and it was of critical importance for survival.

Central's goal was to seek a partnership with a specialist IT&T firm which would provide access to specialised IT solutions. An external provider was believed to offer several advantages over the in-house department. A manager described this:

> The market is changing very dramatically and we do not have the depth in the IT group to be able to provide IT solutions. We wanted to work with a partner whose core business was IT and therefore was in a better position to search the world, to provide us with the right solutions at the right time. Now I do not want to appear to be negative towards our IT groups because they did carry us a long way forward. The question is, did they get too expensive? We lost control of the IT spend, but also the market had moved a lot quicker, and we don't believe the IT groups were dynamic enough to provide the necessary solutions to go forward.

Bring discipline and control to IT&T

A strong motivation for outsourcing was that the use and development of IT within one of the original electricity authorities was out of control. One senior IT manager described the situation that had existed at Hilton:

> In the past, utilities traditionally were fairly wealthy organisations—cash rich and managed predominantly by engineers who like to build gold-plated systems. We

now have redundant microwave links, multiple computer sites, you name it. It was technology gone mad. Whereas the old Woodside was managed by a man whose single focus in life was to build low cost solutions.

In addition, some businesses within Central had started to develop their own IT groups. There was a strong need to bring IT planning and operations under some form of central control.

Criteria used in the outsourcing decision

In mid-1996, Central called for tenders for the IT&T function. Bids from two large global companies were considered, along with a bid from the internal providers. All bidders needed to demonstrate that they could offer value within the changing dynamic electricity environment. The criteria for assessing the tenders included the following:

- cost of providing the service;
- clear cost reduction paths;
- staff transition issues;
- the approach to strategic planning of IT;
- core competencies—what the tenderer could offer in terms of their experience;
- how they planned to manage the contract; and
- the nature of the billing arrangements.

Each criterion was weighted in the final analysis, with the final decision being made by the implementation committee.

The successful tenderer, Global Systems, was chosen for many reasons including its company values, complete proposal, ability to respond speedily to changes in the market, leverage and wide international knowledge base. Other factors which favoured the tenderer were the time-line on cost reduction paths, and the way Global Systems intended to deal with staffing issues. The in-house proposal was said to be 'a clear third' when the three tenders were assessed, largely because the team was unable to provide convincing arguments that it was dynamic enough to provide the necessary IT solutions for the future.

Interestingly, IT staff were not part of the implementation committee as it was felt that they would have too much self-interest in the outcome of the project. Therefore they did not drive the process but were involved and consulted in the decision.

Global Systems was physically located on-site, in the same area as the previous IT&T department of Hilton. Ownership of the information technology machinery and equipment was retained by Central.

Staffing issues

Once the decision was made to outsource IT&T to Global Systems, a team was set up to work with staff on transition issues. Existing IT&T staff were given three choices: take a voluntary redundancy package, transfer their employment to Global Systems, or continue at Central in a different role. About half of the IT&T staff left, the bulk of the remainder transferred to Global Systems, and six employees stayed with Central. Counselling and career transition training were provided for some staff. Many of the employees that transferred to Global Systems saw clear opportunities for career advancement in an organisation that had IT as its core business. Career paths for IT employees within the two electricity authorities had been limited.

Some of the initial problems with the outsourcers related to specialised knowledge about the IT systems 'walking out the door'. As in many companies when redundancy packages are offered, it is often the most talented staff with good employment opportunities who choose to leave. Many of the IT applications at Central were custom-built and not well documented, so often only a single person knew how that software operated. In addition, over time some of Central's IT staff who had transferred to Global Systems moved to other Global sites.

Managing the outsourcing relationship

The first twelve months were described by one manager as 'rocky'. Indeed, it took about eighteen months for positive aspects to clearly emerge. The key issues to manage were:

- agreeing on the 'baseline' level of service to be included in the contract;
- verifying the cost of the baseline services;
- managing false expectations held by staff;
- managing differences between the cultures of Central and Global Systems;
- implementation of communication processes;
- developing trust;
- achieving cost reduction; and
- implementation of the risk/reward scheme.

Agreeing on the baseline

The contract contained an agreed price for baseline services and additional payments for discretionary projects that were above that baseline. Baseline services were defined as '… the cost of maintaining all infrastructure and systems in the organisation at the level at which they were at the point that the contract was signed'. This was very difficult to interpret. In the first year of the contract there were conflicts between Central and Global Systems as each had different ideas as to what constituted baseline services.

These disputes highlighted the criticality of clear specifications in written agreements. A senior manager explained:

> People have to be very clear about their service level requirements. Not say '95 per cent uptime' or something like that. None of this arbitrary nonsense. Be very specific about what those service level requirements are—specify as much as you can get down. And people say 'Oh it's not necessary because you're going to work these things out together'. You can, but that means there needs to be extreme trust and that only occurs when you are really partners. But you do not start as partners. You start with the specifications; you work to it and the supplier–customer relationship. And that is where we came from. In the beginning it was an unhappy customer–supplier relationship.

Some managers believed that these problems could have been averted if more time had been spent carefully negotiating the contract. However, at the time of the merger there was a great sense of urgency to solve the IT problem, and to get an outsourcer on board. The problem in establishing the baseline involved agreeing on which projects were discretionary (over and above baseline services and hence an extra cost to Central) and which projects were included in the baseline service.

Cost verification

Another issue relating to the contract occurred during the first six months of the relationship. Both Global Systems and Central needed to undertake an extensive verification of the cost of baseline services, after the contract was signed. A manager explains why this was the case:

> I would not do that again. With the merger of the organisation, redundancy programs were going on, and with uncertainty in IT staff, there was a need to do something to get some stability in the process. The cost of putting some trust in Global Systems during that 6–9 months process was seen to be less than the cost of delaying and doing the contract verification prior to final contract signing. This was the cost of provision of baseline services. We entered into a contract that basically said, 'This is what we believe it is at the moment, but it will be subject to verification in this next six months'. That should not have occurred. We should have poured it more in concrete. We should have spent more time as a business, chapter and verse, as to what the expectations of service were, what the limitations were, what they were really going to get out of it.

False expectations

In the early days of the relationship many staff at Central were disappointed with Global Systems' performance. There was an expectation that Global Systems would deliver massive improvements in service levels and costs. There were also memories of 'how good things were prior to the partnership'.

Improvements were slow to emerge for a number of reasons. Some of the most valuable IT&T staff had left the company, so the remaining staff did not have the skills to run some of the unique systems. Conflicts emerged from the different objectives of the two parties: the outsourcer was clearly trying to make a good return from the account, while Central was trying to manage costs. It took some time before the two partners were able to work towards shared objectives for various projects. Also, managers within the businesses were now being charged the full costs of their IT&T services, whereas they had previously had much greater direct access to IT&T services and carried few charges.

The decision to outsource IT&T was made within two months of the merger of the two electricity distributors. In itself, this was a difficult blending of two very different cultures. Thus, limited time and attention were given to the details of the contract and to the development of clear expectations about the advantages expected to be gained from the partnership.

Managing two cultures

Central and Global Systems had very different organisational cultures. Central had resulted from the merger of two traditional public sector organisations, but was moving quickly to adopt commercial practices and principles. Global Systems was highly commercial and very militaristic in its operations. One senior manager contrasted the two organisations:

> The way Central works is to have the process in place, but to empower people to do what they need to do. The account is probably worth 40–45 million dollars a year to Global Systems. My equivalent, the number one person in Global Systems, has signing authority to only $5 000—everything else goes up the line and the bureaucracy. You can talk about bureaucracy in the public service, but it is nothing to what you see in the way they control what you can and cannot do. That is the way they work. But having said that, they have introduced a rigour into this organisation, which was far too free with its IT spend. That is a difficult thing to do with an internal IT shop.

After the first eighteen months these differences became less important. One manager believed that this might have been due to Global Systems' 'learning the Central way'.

Communication processes

The manner in which Central related to Global Systems changed over the first two years of the contract. Initially a single manager (Central's IT&T Outsourcing Manager) was the sole contact point for Central, handling all day-to-day problems and trying to build strong relationships. However, the four businesses of Central were distinct and had very different needs and foci. Over time, Global Systems assigned different service managers with responsibility for each business, to handle day-to-day issues directly with those businesses. This allowed the IT&T Outsourcing Manager to focus more on broader relationship issues. A greater focus came to be placed on open communication channels and addressing issues up-front. Once a month senior managers from both Central and Global Systems met as part of an IT steering group, to work through the strategic plan, to discuss major projects and spending to date. There was also a working group to handle applications for new IT capital projects.

Developing trust

The issue of developing trust between Global Systems and Central was seen as important to managers at Central. The managers came to understand that Global Systems was committed to the relationship and a growing basis of trust developed between the two parties. A manager outlined this viewpoint:

> Central still wears by far the biggest risk in this relationship. If you assume the absolute worst, that Global Systems delivers a system late, over budget and with poor quality, sure it might lose out on a couple of million dollars profit, but the cost to Central would be significantly more. So there is an element of trust in this and the trust has to be that Global Systems has a reputation to sustain in the marketplace. It cannot afford to walk away from something like this—and it will not. These large organisations will not and there is a good enough relationship between our CEO and their CEO to ensure that it simply would not happen. There is too much win–win potential to come out of this.

Both parties worked towards building high levels of trust between the two organisations. To that end, where there were incompatibilities, Global Systems replaced some of its staff who were directly involved in the relationships with Central. Among some of the individual businesses within Central, one source of mistrust arose from businesses being charged for IT applications. Some managers felt that Global Systems was 'ripping them off' and engaged in point scoring. The source of this problem, however, was that, for the first time, the businesses were now being charged directly for IT&T services.

The contract with Global Systems was for the provision of management services, while Central continued to own the IT infrastructure. One of the reasons for not giving total control to Global Systems was related to the risk that, if the relationship were to fail with no control over IT assets, it would be difficult to recommence IT services in-house or with another outsourcer. A senior manager explained the relationship between trust and risk.

> The more you trust, the more you are prepared to hand over. The more you feel 'Hey things could break down. What recourse do we have? What backups do we have? Where do we stand in relation to this? How do we rebuild if there is a divorce?' Because of these questions, there's some hesitancy in relation to the ownership of assets—but there's a gradual move away from that thinking.

Managing costs

New management systems were implemented in Central to achieve greater cost control and management of IT developments. Each of the businesses was required to submit an annual plan for new projects. Each project needed to have strong business justifications, and was reviewed by a committee which prioritised the projects. An overall strategic plan for IT, formulated by Central and Global Systems, was developed. This system is a clear contrast to the pre-merger practice of ad hoc project development.

Another aspect that encouraged cost management was the direct charging of IT&T costs to the businesses. These costs were major overhead items that could run to many millions of dollars for each business. The new systems encouraged an environment of accountability and cost consciousness. Managers within the business units began to look for ways that they could break down the costs into manageable elements that people on the shop floor could influence.

The risk/reward scheme

There were no performance measures in the initial outsourcing contract. Eighteen months into the contract, a risk/reward scheme was devised to monitor Global Systems' performance. The first application of this was in relation to a new customer service system (CSS), a discretionary project. The system was developed after several weeks of negotiation between the two parties.

Normally, when Global Systems undertook a discretionary project, it would levy a charge that included direct costs, overhead and profit margin. Under the risk/reward scheme Global Systems would charge only direct costs to Central Energy. Bonuses would then be paid, based on performance in three areas: cost, quality and time. Table 2 provides some examples of the types of measures that were used.

Table 2
Measures used in risk/reward scheme

Criteria	Performance measures	Weightings %
Cost	• Under- or over-budget	25
Quality	• Performance to test plan	20
	• Survey of end users	10
	• Business continuity	20
Time	• Delivery to schedule	25
		100%

Thus, Central awarded Global Systems a score up to 25 based on how prompt they were with delivering the project on time. Depending on how the new system affected business continuity (which might be tested over several months), Global Systems would receive a score of up to 20. (Business continuity was concerned with whether the new system resulted in interruptions to business, such as computer downtime, interrupted access data, and external customer problems.) The targets that were set for each of the performance measures were very challenging. The score that Global Systems received was then linked to a profit multiplier. An overall score of 70 would return a normal profit for the project to Global, whilst a score of 90–100 would give it up to 150 per cent of the normal profit.

Global Systems also conducted its own global customer satisfaction surveys and this data was shared with Central.

Benefits of outsourcing

Managers had high expectations of the improvements that would result from outsourcing the IT&T function to Global Systems. However, benefits were slow to materialise, and it was not until after the first eighteen months of the contract that improvements could be clearly identified by Central's managers. These benefits included:

• access to expertise and enhanced services;
• increased accountability and cost consciousness; and
• a greater discipline in IT planning.

Access to expertise and enhanced services

The new competitive electricity environment placed increased demands on Central Energy to gain access to high IT skills and technologies. There was a strong motivation for outsourcing IT&T and Global Systems was able to provide those benefits to Central. A senior manager described the difference Global Systems made in this area:

> I would also say that they have brought into the organisation, in key areas, skills that we could not have hoped to bring in. The year 2000 problem is a classic case. Their technical headquarters in Australia is in South Australia and they have a big contract with the South Australian government. The skills that they built up there and that they have available to them worldwide are very, very good. They brought two specialists in. We paid big bucks for it, but we got it done in a fraction of the time that it would have taken us to do it internally—to do the reviews, and put the processes in place to allow us to then roll out our Year 2000 plan. The ability to do that and put those processes in place in an internal shop and get the right people for short periods of time—almost impossible!

The association with Global Systems provided Central with the creative IT solutions that it was looking for. Another manager confirmed the importance of Global Systems' international networks:

> And that's the way Global Systems operates, they have a client here, and a client there and if we have a certain issue, what they do is bring someone in. They fly someone in from the States or interstate to solve that specific problem because those people have addressed it before in other organisations.

Accountability and cost consciousness

While IT&T was a major cost for the company, managers at Central were not overly concerned about reducing these costs. Instead, they were more focused on ensuring that the resources were not wasted. To that end, the company put in place new systems to help manage IT activities.

To encourage businesses to use IT responsibly, the cost of the baseline services needed to be redistributed to the businesses which were using the services. A manager explained the philosophy with relation to the 'desktop project', which was a project within the baseline services:

> To sit down around a table with an eighteen–twenty million-dollar baseline service bill and say 'OK, how do we break this up?' is quite a challenge. Hence, what we have agreed to on the desktop project is based on actual charges per desktop per month for a total service. So we're putting the incentive clearly back on the business to manage the number of PCs. Prior to this there's been absolutely no incentive for them to do anything smarter about managing those costs because it

was a lump sum. Now we can say 'If you go from 500 PCs to 350 PCs, you will save yourself $200+ dollars per month'. We have taken a chunk out of the baseline cost and substituted it with a variable cost. As long as the total number of PCs in the organisation does not fall below 1200, these costs will be valid.

The costs of discretionary projects were charged directly to the businesses to which they related. Central, however, was still attempting to develop equitable ways of charging the baseline cost to each business. This activity involved determining the drivers of the cost of discretionary projects. A senior finance manager outlined the difficulties:

We had a subcommittee look at it in several ways, because you are not sure what the cost drivers are. The helpdesk is one of the more expensive items. They decided to just divide the cost equally across the four businesses and holding company. Which means the holding company pays through the neck. We have 30 staff and Contracting has 1200 staff. We have tried to find a reasonable base, and sometimes that was just dividing it equally across all businesses, and that will remain until we have a better understanding of what drives the costs.

As explained in a previous section, each business was required to submit plans of its IT requirements at the start of each year, for approval. This provided control over costs as well as over the ad hoc development of projects that had once existed. Having IT&T managed by an arms-length provider— which itself had strict, bureaucratic systems in place—made the implementation of spending controls simpler and supported Central's attempts to control spending.

Control over ongoing costs was also achieved through the monthly IT charges being managed by the IT&T Outsourcing Manager. All charges were reviewed and checked and only charges for the baseline and approved projects were paid.

Greater discipline in IT planning

Once Global Systems was established as the provider of IT&T, more systematic controls over new IT developments were implemented. Businesses were required to present business justifications for all IT capital projects to the working group. A project would only be approved if there was a strong business justification and if it met the needs across the business.

Lessons learned

The outsourcing of IT&T was seen by managers at Central as an effective response to the problems that existed within its IT&T function. It also provided a foundation for gaining access to IT&T expertise, which was considered essential for competing in the new contestable electricity markets.

IT&T was the first outsourcing contract for Central, and the decision to outsource was undertaken at the time of the merger of the two electricity authorities, in an environment of uncertainty and massive change. The main lessons learned from this outsourcing activity related to the importance of the terms and definitions in the contract. Issues such as the definition of the baseline services, and the need for cost verification dominated the relationship between Central and Global Systems for the first eighteen months of the contract. However, managers at Central realised the importance of putting processes in place to manage the ongoing relationship with the outsourcer. The development of performance indicators to encourage incentives for the outsourcer to deliver projects that met Central's requirements for cost, quality and delivery proved to be an important achievement two years into the contract.

After the merger, Central became involved in the formation of strategic alliances with other suppliers. These alliances were less critical to Central, as they involved less commitment of resources and less dependence compared to the IT&T outsourcing partnership. However, the experiences of the outsourcing activity influenced the processes used to implement the alliances.

A strategic alliance with a cable supplier was undertaken two years after the IT&T contract. This agreement was undertaken without a full written contract—simply a 'heads of agreement'—because the managers negotiating the agreement had experienced the problems that arose with the IT&T contract. There was also a belief that a contract could be a source of mistrust between the company and the supplier. This relationship was characterised by an open book approach to the sharing of information. Performance was tied to risk/return, and a steering committee consisting of managers from both firms developed performance indicators to support areas such as growth, delivery time and cost. A manager described how the new relationship would proceed, compared to the IT&T project:

> It's virtually the same selection process, but we're going to implement it in a different way. We are not going to tie it to a legal contract; we are going to do it using a 'heads of agreement' to try to build it on trust from day one. Now we could fall flat on our face, but some experiences that I've had suggest that the legal agreement does introduce a sense of mistrust from day one, because all the 'i's' have to be dotted and the 't's' have to be crossed. I have to admit our lawyers are not exactly ecstatic about this direction but they have accepted it, with a few additional clauses that we have had to put in to keep them happy. But what we are saying is that we are not going to be tied to a legal agreement. The thing we want to have is an arrangement and partnership built on trust.

The outsourcing of IT&T was seen by managers at Central Energy as an effective response to the problems that existed within its IT&T function. It also provided a foundation for gaining access to IT&T expertise, which was essential for competing in the new contestable electricity markets. The lessons learned from the experience were valuable in influencing the nature of future outsourcing activities, and in particular, in considering the provisions that should be contained within a contract, and even whether or not to enter into a contract as part of a strategic alliance.

4

GREENTREES CITY COUNCIL

Background

Greentrees City Council (Greentrees) is one of the largest local councils in Australia. It has more than 80 000 rateable properties, and approximately 1000 staff. Although the council experienced rapid growth during the 1990s, employee numbers remained constant while the percentage of services provided by contractors increased. The area governed by the council has been identified by Price Waterhouse (now PricewaterhouseCoopers) as one of the top ten business 'hot spots' in Australia in terms of average population growth, high retail sales, above average disposable income, strong housing commencements and low unemployment. Land is reasonably priced and only 60 per cent of the land area is developed.

Greentrees is a multi-purpose council, providing a wide range of services which includes the construction and maintenance of recreation facilities (such as parks and aquatic centres), road construction and maintenance, animal management, childcare facilities and recycling services. Greentrees is located in New South Wales, where local councils tend to be closely aligned with political parties. This can influence a council's strategic direction and decisions.

Unlike in Victoria, local councils in New South Wales are not compelled to tender all services for outsourcing. Rather, councils are expected to 'defend their position and justify actions that they take'. It is important that any outsourcing decisions are justifiable and based on a valid consideration of all costs and benefits.

Types of outsourcing

The two main areas of outsourcing at Greentrees were road and bridge construction and maintenance, and parks maintenance. Other areas that were considered for outsourcing included a childcare centre, a leisure centre and recycling services. Areas that were not outsourced included services that would not be considered very attractive to outside suppliers (that is, there were not large profit margins in the provision of those services), including the installation of road signs, seats and bus shelters.

The Engineering Department managed the design, maintenance and construction of roads, bridges and drainage. Over the past 20 years this type of work has been increasingly undertaken by outside contractors. Indeed, in-house staff now carry out only 35 per cent of construction work—down from 80 per cent 20 years ago. At the same time, the number of workers employed by the council in these areas remained constant. In many situations in-house employees worked alongside contractors on projects.

Motivation for outsourcing

In the mid-1990s, Greentrees decided to reduce its internal labour force so that approximately half the city's parks were maintained by internal labour, and the other half by external service providers. There were two reasons for this. First, Greentrees did not want to lose its own expertise in the area; and second, it provided the opportunity to measure internal performance (in respect to cost and quality) against external service providers.

The environment of local government councils changed dramatically in the 1990s, as councils came under increasing pressure to be more market-oriented and cost-effective. These aspects were the main motivations underlying the move towards increased outsourcing by Greentrees. These pressures also created some confusion for many people working in this sector. A senior council manager explained the changes:

> There is no doubt that local government as an industry is changing—its whole role is being questioned. It definitely has a role, but the problem is determining exactly what that role is. Also, there are now efficient markets that never used to exist. A lot of what we deliver was determined by the old public good argument, and the fact that nobody else was able to deliver it. That's not the case any more: the private sector has been looking for new markets and found them, and technology has

meant that they can deliver things that they could not before, at a reasonable price. This means that local government has had to break down the inflexibility that used to be there and become a more flexible organisation, and move out of some services that it used to think were its sole domain and move into others. And that in itself is proving very challenging and has led to the need to review the service delivery argument.

Thus, new opportunities were emerging in the market place, which could be used by councils such as Greentrees to improve cost performance.

Criteria used in outsourcing decisions

Greentrees has been involved in a number of outsourcing decisions over the last twenty years. In particular, the outsourcing of road construction and maintenance commenced in the early 1980s. The criteria that Greentrees considered in making outsourcing decisions included the following:

- whether the activity was core to the business;
- whether there were opportunities in the external market for the service;
- the cost and quality of the potential outsourcers;
- the desire to maintain in-house expertise; and
- philosophical considerations of what should, and should not be outsourced.

Core activities

Consistent with other organisations, Greentrees sought only to outsource areas of the business that it identified as non-core. Activities identified as core to the business included statutory reporting, corporate development, the strategic directorate, and the IT function. Clearly, some of these functions (particularly IT) are outsourced in many organisations, which demonstrates that determining which functions are strategically important varies by organisation. Despite many years of experience, managers at Greentrees found that determining what was non-core remained difficult.

Market opportunities

The council was involved in offering hundreds of different types of services and, in such an environment, it was difficult to determine where opportunities existed for outsourcing. An interesting aspect of the service sector, in which Greentrees was involved, was that external organisations were continually creating new markets. A manager explained:

There are new markets growing up in the economy all of the time—new businesses that people are inventing for themselves that provide you with an opportunity to get it done internally or outsource it. And to actually stay in touch with all those markets and to be aware of them all—and then to be able to apply them to your own organisation—is difficult. We are trying to facilitate line management to take on this role. At present there are cultural challenges and training challenges as well. In an organisation this big and devoted to keeping its overheads down, expanding your corporate development unit so it can reach through an organisation of this size, and also stay in touch with the market options—that's quite a big job! And I know that we have not got the answer to this. It is very much a constant perusal of the next things that we can look at and reconsider. The management information and systems are there, and I think the commitment to achieving the most cost-effective result for the council is there, but if you don't get line management involved, it simply is not going to work.

Cost and quality

Cost effectiveness was a driver of the move to outsource services, so it was an important consideration in the decision making process. Out-of-pocket costs, transaction costs and opportunity costs were all considered by managers in the cost analyses. A manager explained:

In our analyses we would take into account the contract charges, plus any costs associated with or incurred by us in administering the contract (insurance-related costs, that sort of thing) and compare this with the cost of our providing the service internally. At the end of the day there are certain costs we have distributed or allocated that will not necessarily go away if we make an outsourcing decision. Things like this building we work in. We could build in property rent but unless we have made a strategic decision to turn around and market that space for rent, we have not really incurred those cost savings. You see what I mean? There could be an opportunity cost, or we could expand an area of our operation and make use of that space.

In the evaluation process it was important for tenderers to demonstrate that they were financially stable. However, the tenderers also needed to demonstrate they could provide services of high quality and sustain a consistent level of service:

This organisation is very conscious of the fact that the cheapest price is not necessarily the best, and we need to ensure that the level of quality and quantity of service delivery is there. Also, the external tenderers must have the ability to sustain a consistent level of service. We need to know that we are not going to be turning around in six months' time and going to tender again because the contractor has become insolvent—which has happened on numerous occasions. They have to prove their financial stability to us. Believe me, we are not experts. We are still very, very new. The engineering area is probably the most advanced in terms of contract administration and being able to specify in their contracts clearly the level and quality of service that they expect.

In some areas there were recognised quality standards that tenderers had to meet. For example, childcare standards were needed to retain a childcare licence, so outsourcers needed to demonstrate that they could meet those required standards.

Maintaining in-house expertise

Decisions to outsource services were not based solely on cost and quality criteria. In some situations, managers considered it important to retain expertise or intellectual investment in a particular area. This came from a realisation that in the future there may always be the need to take a service back in-house. A manager described the issue:

> It comes down to what the council perceives its role to be. If you take this current management team and this current council, there are things that we deem to be strategically important in which we would never want to lose our intellectual property or investment. We need to safeguard the long-term ability of this organisation to be effective—things like the financial planning, and head office control of the organisation.

In line with this principle, many services within Greentrees were undertaken by a mix of internal staff and external contractors.

Philosophical considerations

Another aspect which influenced outsourcing decisions at Greentrees was the prevailing 'philosophy' of the elected council members. That is, the elected councillors may believe that there are certain services that the council should provide to residents, despite cost considerations. In the decision about whether or not to outsource the childcare centre, an influential argument was that Greentrees had a duty to provide affordable childcare to its constituents —this is the 'public good' argument. These viewpoints were reflected in the mission statement of the council.

The evaluation process

Greentrees formed a Tender Evaluation Committee to examine whether tenders complied with relevant legislation, and to review the service provider's performance against standards specified in the contract. To this end, some areas within Greentrees developed a list of preferred contractors who had demonstrated a greater awareness of the desired level of service and timeliness.

A well-established tender evaluation process was used in the engineering department and for parks maintenance. Contracts for road construction and maintenance were usually for two–four years, and called for by tender.

Managers used the Australian Consulting Engineers Association's list of selection criteria, which included measures of unit rates, prior performance, professionalism, and administrative set-up. Prior performance might relate to work undertaken for Greentrees or for another business. An engineering manager elaborated the criteria that were considered when comparing tenders:

> We include such things as the professionalism of the company. We look at its administration set-up, office set-up, facilities, and whether it has computer back-up for its progress payment claims. We look to see if it has a good safety record, whether it has a safety plan within the organisation to meet Workcover requirements. It's no use getting in a 'fly-by-night bloke' who puts in low prices, does a lousy job and we end up having trouble with him for the next 12 months, or two or three years. We do not necessarily go for the cheapest. We then have a tender review committee that is made up of different officers from different departments. They get a list of all the tenders, the rates submitted, the selection process that was followed and reasons for the recommendation and successful tenderers. If necessary, they interview people involved in the selection process and once they're happy with it they sign off on it and the report then goes to council which endorses the selection of these tenderers. That puts the councillors at ease. They feel that there is a transparency in the selection process. We report our recommendation, and the basis for it, to council.

Developing internal tenders

Like all Australian local councils, Greentrees followed the guidelines of the Commonwealth Government's *Competitive Neutrality Policy Statement* (1996). In New South Wales, competitive tendering is not compulsory. Rather, councils are required to determine in which situations it is of benefit to tender out services. These decisions must be capable of standing up to independent scrutiny. Probity provisions also require a separation between those parts of the business involved in the decision to outsource and those sections that are involved in internal tenders. Internal and external tenderers must compete on an equal footing for those areas defined as 'category one businesses' under the competitive policy requirements. A manager explained the approach:

> Many of the various businesses are in direct competition with external providers of that service. Our view was that we had to actually be out there, taking market share from other providers. You know, it's a bit like building your own house. If you want to go owner-builder, well that's fine—you are only competing if you want to turn around and build other people's houses. So that was our philosophy. Now we turn anywhere between five and twenty million dollars a year in land development and that is in direct competition to other land developers. Childcare and aquatic facilities are further examples.

In many outsourcing decisions considered by Greentrees, internal service providers developed tenders. Competitive neutrality was preserved through the creation of a separate section of the finance department of the council, which assisted in the preparation of internal bids. This section was at arms-length from the other section of finance which was responsible for helping management choose between an internal and external bid. The council's activity-based costing (ABC) models were used to prepare the information for the internal bid, and discounted cash flow analysis was used to extend the analysis over a five or ten year period.

Examples of outsourcing decisions

Three examples of the decision making process are discussed below. These decisions relate to a leisure facility, a childcare centre and recycling services.

Leisure facility

One outsourcing decision faced by the council related to whether or not to outsource a council-managed leisure facility. The primary factors considered in this decision were cost and control.

Greentrees used an ABC system to measure and control costs. The process with regard to costs was to measure the out-of-pocket costs that would be incurred if a project was outsourced (including administration and insurance costs), and compare these to the cost of the project if it were conducted in-house by the council. Opportunity costs were included in the cost analysis. A discounted cash flow analysis, over a five-year period, was also undertaken.

In the case of the leisure facility, Greentrees also evaluated the decision in light of its desire to retain internal management, and thus control, of the facility. The council received tenders to manage the facility (including an internal tender). In the end result, the decision was clear-cut, as the successful tender involved the external group *paying* Greentrees \$40 000–\$50 000 a year to manage the facility.

Childcare facility

Another outsourcing decision addressed by the council was whether or not to outsource a childcare facility. Greentrees was a substantial provider of childcare, with a number of childcare centres under its control. The management committee of one centre disbanded, leaving Greentrees with the decision of whether to continue to run the facility itself, or to outsource.

There were two competing arguments in this decision. The argument in favour of outsourcing was financial, and centred around the premise that

Greentrees was in the childcare business to earn profits—yet, in this case, profits were not being generated. The alternative argument was that Greentrees was under political pressure to provide affordable childcare to its constituents—the 'public good' argument. While the management of the childcare facility was put to tender, the public good argument eventually held sway, and Greentrees continued to manage the facility itself. Quality of service was another important consideration in this decision, particularly as a new accreditation system for childcare facilities had emerged.

Recycling services

Decisions concerning the recycling services provide another interesting insight into Greentrees' decision making processes on outsourcing. In 1988, Cleanbins was successful in winning the tender for the recycling services. However, after two years, Cleanbins was unable to provide the service at the tendered cost. The contract went out to tender, and an internal bid from Greentrees was successful. This tender was not the cheapest, but there were concerns over the ability of external providers to provide a consistent, continuous service. The ability to do this was a major factor in Greentrees' outsourcing decision, particularly as it had experienced problems in the past with external service providers becoming insolvent. As a result, the ability of an external service provider to supply a continuous, consistent level of service was measured both quantitatively (in terms of financial viability) and qualitatively.

Managing the outsourcing relationship

Three main issues emerged as important in managing the outsourcing contracts at Greentrees City Council:

- specifying service standards;
- responsibility for occupational health and safety; and
- performance reviews.

Specifying service standards

An important aim for managers at Greentrees was to develop partnerships, or close relationships, with outsourcers. As contracts were renewed or new ones written, levels of required service came to be more clearly specified. This was made easier to achieve by identifying standards for measuring levels of service, particularly in relation to public liability and occupational health and safety issues. According to a senior council manager, the key in outsourcing was to develop relationships:

Developing a relationship with a provider that's going to work with you in the long term and has a vested interest and wants to maintain more than one contract with you—and working with those people to set standards that they think are achievable and satisfy what we want to deliver for the rate payers is another part that I think we can work on more actively. The road construction area has matured a lot and has that type of relationship with most of the people, but there a few other areas, which are newer, and I don't know if they actually pursue it as much.

Occupational health and safety

Over the years, Greentrees came to realise that it had responsibilities for the employees of contractors that extended to occupational health and safety and public liability. A manager explained this idea:

Just because it is a third party, you are not removed from your obligations under occupational health and safety, public liability and workers compensation. You are just as liable as you would be managing your own people. That may seem obvious. But many people think you are outsourcing the function and that you no longer have the responsibility. But you have not walked away from the responsibility. You are still the person facilitating the delivery of that service. Therefore, skills are required in how you actually manage and negotiate with the contractor and how you build those things into the contract to safeguard the council's interest.

In the engineering department, managers worked hard to convince contractors of the importance of complying with safety requirements:

If our contractors are doing things that are unsafe, not only do the contractors get hit with the ramifications; we, the council, are also responsible as we supervise the project. We have put out a folder with all the Workcover documents. It has a CD that identifies all the courses that Workcover are running — it has brochures on everything from skin cancer right through to ear muffs — and we present it to each contractor and say 'It doesn't matter how big or small you are, you must comply with these requirements'. Some companies say 'But I've been doing this job for 50 years' and we say 'Sorry, but you won't be doing it for another 50 years unless you comply'. Quite a few of them say, 'I'm too old to change but I'll employ this man and he will make sure we comply.' So for $50 000 a year he is now confident that his company is complying with all the safety requirements. They have achieved what we set out for them.

Performance reviews

Whether a project was completed by in-house employees or a contractor, there was always a review undertaken. The review included a series of checklists, including safety criteria. For example, in the road building area the quality of the design was reviewed and performance measures developed to indicate the costs of poor design quality. (These are the costs of correcting problems or redesigning a project due to poor design.) An engineering manager provided some examples:

> The level may be wrong on the plans and the people working suddenly find out, or the pipelines have been laid and all of a sudden there's a pipe going the opposite way—and then you've got to go back and remove the pipe and do redesign work. It does not happen that often, but it is a measure of poor design. And we do the same thing through the construction process. With a contractor, if it is their mistake, they wear it. If it is caused by bad instructions from us, or our bad design, then we have to pay them.

In the case of some large lump-sum contracts, bonuses or penalties attach to meeting certain deadlines. This condition aimed to provide incentives for projects to be completed on time, and also to cover situations where it could cost the council extra money when deadlines are missed. For example, the construction of a bridge across a railway line required that there was no activity on the railway during the last stage of the construction. If the railway shutdown did not occur on a particular weekend, the council would have incurred considerable additional costs. Thus, a major bonus (or penalty) was offered to the contractor dependent on the last stage of construction being completed (or not completed) by that particular weekend.

In evaluating tenders for parks maintenance, Greentrees found, in some instances, that the internal providers were not as cost-effective as external providers. However, there were sometimes serious problems with external providers, first, in terms of financial stability, and second, in terms of the quality of their service. Quality was assessed in terms of their ability to cut and maintain grass to an expected level. A manager explained:

> We'd set quite a high level for quality because of the internal providers, and we expected that for the whole city, and because of the nature of the external providers —you know coming from another type of organisation or just taking up lawn mowing—they come in with a low price and think they can do it with a couple of lawn mowers when they really need big slashers and all sorts of things. So they find themselves unable to maintain that level of service—which is a three-inch high cut throughout the whole year. Therefore, over the years we have been able to develop quite a good mix, and found a few quite good contractors, by being able to carry out the direct comparison between the two forms of providers. Our own day labour force has been very receptive to that and we've been able to introduce some great workplace agreements that have enabled us to reduce the cost of those internal units down to the equivalent of the external providers. And at the same time bring the quality of the external providers up to that of the internal providers. So that has worked very well.

Benefits of outsourcing

Greentrees was able to identify several benefits from outsourcing. Outsourcing services allowed the council to:

- benchmark internal performance against external service providers;
- focus on priorities; and
- achieve flexibility in service provision.

Benchmarking internal performance

The mix of internal and external service providers gave Greentrees the opportunity to benchmark all its providers. For example, in areas such as engineering services and parks maintenance, contractors worked alongside in-house employees, which allowed for direct performance comparisons. In the engineering department, the cost of contractors was continually benchmarked against the cost of employees. Generally, the cost of internal staff was very competitive. However, if internal staff were not quite as cost-effective as the contracted staff, they might still be retained. This gave the council flexibility as some jobs were difficult to contract, and internal staff were often needed as an 'urgent response resource' to assist in emergencies such as flooding.

In some situations—such as in parks maintenance, where internal staff were not as cost-effective as the contractors—new workplace enterprise agreements were introduced which focused on improving cost performance.

Focus on priorities

The services that councils such as Greentrees are expected to deliver to their residents are extensive. Managers in Greentrees identified 80 different groups of services that it provided. By outsourcing some services to 'expert' providers, managers were able to focus their attention on fewer, more critical activities. As a manager explained:

> One of the real benefits of outsourcing is that, to a certain extent, it allows you to focus—particularly in a local authority, which is very diverse in terms of what they deliver—on a lesser number of things and hopefully deliver a better quality of service.

Flexibility

Outsourcing helped the council handle the peaks and troughs that occurred in its business. Many tasks in the construction area were specialised, and the demand for these specialists was not continuous. For example, curb and gutter specialists might only be needed for three days in a six-week project. Thus, it was not efficient to employ staff for those tasks, as they would only be occupied part of the time. Other examples of specialised services contracted out were concrete restoration and maintenance. Companies that specialised in these areas were contracted for two or three years and, depending on the task, were given either a yearly program of required work, or two–three weeks' notice before they were required.

Lessons learned

Greentrees Council has evaluated and managed outsourcing contracts, particularly in the road construction and maintenance area, for many years. The experience that it gained over this period resulted in many modifications and the streamlining of procedures.

A distinctive aspect of Greentrees' outsourcing practices is the mixing of both internal and external contractors, sometimes on the one project. Over time, this allowed the council to benchmark internal and external performance. As new contracts came to be written, levels of service came to be more tightly specified, making it easier to evaluate performance.

Initially, a prime criterion for evaluating tenders for outsourcing contracts was out-of-pocket cost. In time, Greentrees came to include a broader range of cost criteria in its outsourcing decisions, including transaction costs and opportunity costs. In addition, criteria such as service quality and the occupational health and safety practices of the provider became increasingly important. This was explained by a senior manager:

> In the early days you outsourced non-core responsibilities and non-core functions and from my observations a lot of outsourcing decisions were based around raw cost data, without any of the considerations that come back and bite you later on. And I suppose we all learned from that and adjust our costings and thinking accordingly, to take into account a more complete picture of whether in fact it is better to outsource or not.

5

ELECTNET

Background

ElectNet was formed to manage a high voltage electricity transmission network. It had previously formed part of a larger organisation, Power Co. (Power), which was responsible for electricity generation and distribution, and which retained responsibility for those activities after the separation. ElectNet's major customers are electricity distributors, who then on-sell to consumers and large business customers. As with Central Energy, deregulation of the Australian electricity industry has led to increased competition for ElectNet and, at the same time, provided the company with a potentially broader customer base through access to customers in other Australian states.

The outsourcing decision

The function that forms the focus of this case is information technology (IT). The outsourcing decision, however, is different to that of the other organisations described in this study in that ElectNet was not faced with a decision of whether to outsource or retain the function in-house. When ElectNet was split from Power, information technology services continued to be provided by the IT department of Power. However, it quickly became obvious to ElectNet that this was far from an ideal situation and that, given the urgency of acquiring a high quality stand-alone IT facility, outsourcing was the only alternative.

However, it was not considered feasible to complete a tendering process in a short period so the company, for the time being, continued to use the services of Power and engaged essential strategic suppliers on a time and materials basis to assist in providing necessary IT services.

Despite the time pressures, ElectNet took a cautious approach to outsourcing the IT function, as management was conscious of the potential problems that could accompany the appointment of an unsuitable outsourcer. Over a two-year period, managers within ElectNet undertook a considerable amount of research to prepare for the tendering process. As an IT manager explained:

> We wanted to be confident that we were on the right track. We acknowledged that we were on a learning curve as far as managing outsourcing was concerned. We spent a lot of time investigating other outsourced arrangements and learning from that. It was at a time when more and more outsourcing was being undertaken in Australia. I spoke at a large number of conferences on what we had been learning, and sought input from other organisations. We joined an outsourcing management group that Gartner Consulting ran and we were very active in the industry. Our contract became really a hybrid contract of picking up the good things that we thought we had learnt during that time.

Eventually, the decision was made to outsource software support and hardware support to two separate outsourcers. At the time of making the decision to outsource, ElectNet owned its own computer hardware, and ownership was retained after outsourcing.

Motivation for outsourcing

The three interrelated reasons for outsourcing the IT function were:

- the desire to create a distinct IT strategy;
- the inability of the existing supplier to meet the changing IT needs of ElecNet; and
- the need to gain access to high calibre IT skills.

Creation of a distinct IT strategy

While ElectNet had the option to retain Power as the provider of IT services, it preferred to develop its own distinctive IT strategy to support its distinctive mission. Under the arrangements with Power, ElectNet did not have control over the IT strategy and found it difficult to gain the service provision and outcomes it desired.

Inability of the current provider to service ElecNet's needs

A further reason for tendering IT services was a belief among ElectNet management that, in the future, Power would not be in a position to service the new organisation's specific needs. The business of Power was changing and moving into areas that were very different to those of ElectNet. Indeed, it was doubtful whether Power would be willing to configure itself to adequately manage the changing IT needs of ElectNet's business.

Thus, the decision to outsource the IT function was based on the desire of the company to develop its own distinct approach to managing IT that would reflect the specific needs of an electricity transmission business. This would also allow the company to gain full control over its IT function, which was considered important for the efficient delivery of its services.

Access to high-calibre skills

Although an IT function could have been created in-house, managers at ElectNet felt the need for access to high-calibre IT skills. As a medium-sized organisation, it believed that it would be difficult to attract such specialists to an in-house IT department because of the lack of a sufficiently attractive career path. However, information systems were essential to delivering high voltage transmission services, so the issue of whether such a critical service should be outsourced was also considered. Reconciling these two views, one manager explained:

> Our core competencies are in how we apply our IT systems to be more effective in high-voltage transmission service delivery. So it is really the application of the systems to our business that is important, not what goes on at the back end.

Criteria used in the outsourcing decision

After two years of research, ElectNet called for tenders. Several suppliers were approached and five criteria were used to assess the tenders. These were as follows:

- the skills of the individuals that the outsourcer would bring to the project;
- the extent of corporate experience in providing similar outsourcing services;

- the ability of the outsourcer to draw on its own wider corporate resources to service ElectNet's requirements;
- appropriate quality control and delivery procedures (for example, provision of a helpdesk); and
- cost.

In evaluating tenders, ElectNet considered the individual skills of senior employees of the outsourcer who would form the dedicated IT team. It was felt to be very important that the team had the set of skills necessary to support the IT operations. Another criterion related to the outsourcer having access to a broad set of skills within its own organisation and thus be able to provide additional expertise whenever the need arose. Notably, while cost was a consideration and a cost/benefit analysis was undertaken as part of the tendering process, it was not the prime criterion or motivator of the outsourcing decision.

Ultimately, two outsourcers were engaged: one to manage the operation of the hardware, and another to manage the provision of software services.

Managing the outsourcing relationship

ElectNet put considerable effort into developing the initial contracts with the outsourcers as it believed that this was key to managing the outsourcing relationships. The first twelve months were difficult for all parties, partially because a short handover period did not allow the outsources adequate preparation time.

Issues that were relevant to the management of the outsourcers included:

- managing the handover process;
- specification in the contracts;
- performance measurement;
- monthly meetings;
- staffing issues; and
- achieving business alignment.

The handover process

Over a six-week period, control over IT was handed from Power to the outsourcers. The handover period was a difficult time for ElectNet, as it was felt that Power took a 'letter-of-the-law' approach, rather than a value-adding approach. One manager at ElectNet described it as '… one of the most difficult times in my life.' The outsourcers also experienced difficulty as the handover period was insufficient to allow them to accumulate the knowledge necessary to develop their own stand-alone IT function.

Specifications in the contracts

ElectNet decided to separate the outsourcing of software and hardware. The holder of the software support contract was responsible for providing support for operations. This included tasks such as operating ElectNet's helpdesk, maintenance of the desktop computers, and software upgrades. ElectNet retained ownership of the software.

The holder of the hardware support contract provided facilities management. While the outsourcer could advise ElectNet on issues such as hardware replacement, the ultimate decision for hardware acquisition remained with the company.

The two contracts included a number of important points, which were formulated during the two-year period before the calling of tenders:

- Commitment to the vision and values of ElectNet.
- Co-operation. There needed to be a commitment on the part of the outsourcers to work co-operatively across the various contracts.
- Systems audits. The outsourcer was to complete systems audits as part of the contract.
- Systems integration. While initially the outsourcers were to deliver a range of discrete services, over time a more holistic approach to service provision was desired.

Two main elements were covered under these contracts—day-to-day operations, and minor project work. Major projects were not included as ElectNet preferred to 'go to the market' for any new major IT project work. ElectNet also contracted with an external organisation for financial software.

Performance measurement

Two types of service levels were used by ElectNet to evaluate the outsourcers' performance—core level and specific level. Core service levels were embedded into contracts. In the hardware support contract, for example, core measures included availability and reliability. Other specific measures were negotiated from time to time, but were not included in contracts. ElectNet's IT manager considered that specific service level measures were not difficult to negotiate:

> We try to take a partnership approach with our service providers so that, for the majority of the time, both sides have the same interest in making the thing work and being successful.

Financial incentives were not built into contracts, with ElectNet instead preferring to provide non-financial incentives, such as offering to act as a reference site for the outsourcer. Furthermore, flexibility was factored into contracts, allowing ElectNet the opportunity to re-negotiate contracts if significant changes took place.

Monthly meetings

Monthly service review meetings were held with both outsourcers to review performance against service targets. These meetings provided the opportunity for feedback between the outsourcers and ElectNet, and allowed for the identification and resolution of issues. The software outsourcer had regular meetings with the systems' owners throughout ElectNet to ensure that services were appropriately delivered at the right level. The hardware outsourcer met ElectNet on each site to consider any infrastructure issues.

Staffing issues

ElectNet began with only a single staff member managing the interface between the company and the IT outsourcers. An IT team was gradually established within the company and over time became responsible for IT strategy, contract management, IT purchasing and training. ElectNet was allowed some input into senior appointments within the IT team, who were employed by the outsourcing companies.

Achieving business alignment

The achievement of a close business alignment between ElectNet and the outsourcers was seen to be important in creating a smooth working relationship. This included the need for the outsourcers to gain an understanding of how the business operated and an appreciation of the values of ElectNet. Some initial problems were experienced as the outsourcers were not familiar with the company's business cycles. One manager explained the difficulty of conveying the nature of the business to the outsourcers:

> The thing you realise is that the benefit of an internal in-house team is that they actually participate in the business processes. An internal group has to do its own budget so it realises, as well as everyone else, that it is important to have the budget system available at a certain time. You do not need to tell them because they are doing it. Now the outsourcers obviously are not part of this process. And so it is important to focus on communication ... while a lot of stuff is written down in documentation, you've really got to learn it through communication and experience.

Managers at ElecNet considered that ongoing communication with the outsourcers was crucial to achieve that business alignment.

Benefits of outsourcing

At the time of writing this report, ElectNet had four years' experience with the outsourcing of IT, and managers believed that sound and supportive relationships were being established. Nevertheless, during the first year, it was a struggle for all parties: new staff needed to be recruited, and new software applications and new hardware were introduced. After twelve months, clear benefits began to emerge for ElectNet. These benefits included:

- improved service provision;
- improved accountability;
- an increase in control; and
- the development of new management skills.

Improved service provision

Before the establishment of ElectNet as a separate entity, there was some dissatisfaction with the services provided by the IT department of Power.

Power's IT department had been perceived as having 'a life of its own'. This may have been due to the fact that it was considered a profit centre within Power. The IT department was under pressure to 'earn money' from the rest of the organisation. This led to the department developing and providing high levels of customised products to departments within Power and to ElectNet. As one manager stated:

> IT was a profit centre and that encouraged the type of behaviour where the more products they could sell you and roll out, the more money they would make. So they were quite open to customisation and to meeting the most specific requirements, because there was a buck in it for them.

By comparison, the outsourcers were said to have a sharper focus on IT service delivery. Levels of customisation were lower and customer satisfaction, which was measured formally through regular customer service surveys within the organisation, indicated improvement.

Management believed that the use of a contract assisted in ensuring that the outsourcer had a strong customer focus. However, the commercial reality of the contract was that the outsourcer also aimed to earn a profit. Managers at ElectNet worked to attempt to balance these often-conflicting objectives.

Improved IT accountability

There was a belief among managers at ElectNet that the outsourcing of IT resulted in:

- an increased discipline towards the entire process of IT service provision; and
- a desired increase in the availability of technical skills.

The outsourcing of IT also improved accountability in terms of IT development. The move from internal to external sourcing seemed to underlie this change. As ElectNet's financial controller stated:

> I suppose the old IT group did have a life of its own in some ways. In ElectNet, the strategy is ours. We've driven it and we'll take a stand on new applications. We will not customise and maybe because it's not internal billing, maybe because it's real dollars going out the door, we take a much more closer look at proposed IT changes.

Improved control

As discussed in Chapter 1, it is often claimed that a loss of control may occur when an organisation outsources a function. This potential loss of control is usually perceived as being a disadvantage of outsourcing. ElectNet's experience was different, however. Both the IT manager, who was responsible for managing the outsourcing process, and the financial controller believed that control actually *increased* as a result of outsourcing. The IT manager explained:

> I came to the view that control actually increases because of the contractual/performance management focus that you give it. People say that one of the risks of outsourcing is that you lose control. Well, in fact, control increases because you are applying this formal process to service delivery and better performance management, that you are not applying to your internal teams.

Despite this, both the IT manager and the financial controller at ElectNet conceded that the control issue may have been seen differently if ElectNet had not retained its own hardware. The IT manager made the following comments:

> We deliberately decided to retain ownership of the hardware. We wanted to maximise our flexibility in the process and our view was if we sold the hardware off to the outsourcer—what if we get disaffected with them? Or what if someone we don't like buys this computer company, then where do we stand? All of a sudden we are dealing with a whole new ball game—they own the equipment. So our view was that in order to maximise our flexibility and make it easier to make changes, we would retain ownership of the hardware and the software.

The development of new management skills

Another cited benefit of the outsourcing process at ElectNet was the development of management skills—that is, the IT group within ElectNet developed the ability to manage an outsourced entity. Interestingly, the IT manager found that these types of skills were similar to those which should be used in managing internal service delivery.

Lessons learned

ElectNet spent considerable time at the start of the outsourcing activity researching other companies' experiences and considering how outsourcers could be managed. Nevertheless, there were still some areas where the company would have acted differently if it had to undertake the process again.

The initial handover process from Power was a difficult process for ElectNet to manage. In retrospect, the IT manager felt that Power could have provided more support as part of the handover of responsibilities to the outsourcers. The IT manager also suggested that it may have been worthwhile to engage an external company to manage the handover process on ElectNet's behalf, but noted that such companies have only emerged in recent times.

ElectNet believed that an important issue in establishing a successful relationship with outsourcers was the achievement of an organisational or cultural fit between it and the outsourcer. While this is very difficult to specify in a contract, ElectNet's management thought it possible to consider 'fit' to some extent during the initial tender evaluation process. A manager explained:

> You come to understand the culture of outsourcers through your own investigations. You can also ask for references on the tenderers. So it is possible to factor cultural fit into the evaluation criteria.

Another area in which the management of the outsourcing relationship improved over the course of the contract was in the increased sophistication of the monthly reporting system. Over time, ElectNet's understanding of what it required from the outsourcers improved. Consequently, the company became better equipped to identify exactly what it wanted to know about performance. The IT manager at ElectNet considered that the value of the monthly reporting system improved significantly.

The engagement of the outsourcers led to improved control and the development of new skills that were required to manage the outsourced IT function. However, these skills could conceivably have been developed when IT was an in-house activity:

> That is one of the learnings that I took away. In fact, the skills that you develop in managing an outsourced supply are probably skills that you should be applying to internal service delivery. I can look back on this because I was the manager of an internal service delivery team in the old Power IT group, and it struck me how valuable that approach would have been to internal service delivery.

ElectNet is now considering outsourcing other functions of its business. Recently, the organisation outsourced its maintenance function. The organisation's IT outsourcing experiences were considered too dissimilar from maintenance outsourcing to provide assistance. However, fleet outsourcing is being considered by the organisation, and managers believe that the IT outsourcing experiences could provide a suitable model.

6

KEY THEMES AND CONCLUSIONS

In this final chapter, the four case studies are revisited to distil common themes that emerged in the outsourcing experiences, and to answer the two research questions: What are the important issues that must be managed within an outsourcing relationship? Is it more difficult to control an outsourced activity, compared to an in-house function? First, the similarities and differences between the four firms' outsourcing experiences are described. This is followed by a summary of the motivation for outsourcing, the criteria used by each firm to make its outsourcing decisions, and the benefits experienced by the four firms. The section on the management of outsourcing relationships forms the main part of the chapter, which ends with a consideration of control of an outsourced function.

Four contrasting case studies

The four case studies present varying outsourcing situations. Gradient outsourced various operational functions that were formerly undertaken by employees. The contractors were specialist firms that were resident on-site and interacted closely with Gradient's employees. Following a merger of two electricity distributors, Central outsourced its information technology operations, rather than relying on the existing information technology functions of the two former organisations. Greentrees outsourced a variety of functions, while continuing to undertake some of the same functions in-house, so that outsourcers' employees worked alongside in-house staff. On its formation, ElectNet engaged an outsourcer to manage its information technology, rather than build its own IT capabilities.

While cases outlined in this study indicate different outsourcing experiences, there are also similarities. Gradient and Greentrees had extensive experience with outsourcing many aspects of their businesses, and had become accustomed to the employees of outsourcers working on-site, alongside internal employees. Gradient outsourced functions that were critical to the success of its production processes. Greentrees needed to marry commercial justifications with 'public good' considerations in making some of its outsourcing decisions. Both Central and ElectNet engaged in large contracts for the outsourcing of information technology services. These services were critical to enabling these firms to compete effectively within the new contestable electricity environment. It took Central about two years to clarify and establish a good working relationship with its outsourcer. Similarly, ElectNet had a rocky start to its relationships with its outsourcers, following a brief handover period.

Within each of the four organisations, the following issues were considered:

- What motivated the firm to consider outsourcing?
- What criteria were used to evaluate the outsourcing decision?
- What were the benefits gained from outsourcing?
- What lessons emerged from the outsourcing experience?

The findings from the four case studies are summarised in the following sections. In this chapter, we also consider issues that relate to the management of the outsourcing relationship:

- What are the important issues that must be managed within an outsourcing relationship?
- Is it more difficult to control an outsourced activity, compared to an in-house function?

Motivation for outsourcing

The factors that motivated each of the four firms to engage in outsourcing are summarised in Table 3. Clearly, cost management or cost effectiveness was a strong motivation in all organisations, other than ElectNet. In the case of Central, however, the focus was not so much on cost cutting, but on the efficient management of financial resources. Access to specialised skills and expertise were not important at Greentrees, as this organisation had expertise in the areas that were outsourced. In contrast, at Central, Gradient and ElectNet, outsourcers were sought to provide expertise and specialised skills not available in-house.

Table 3
Factors that motivated the decision to outsource

Factors	Gradient Steel	Central Energy	Greentrees Council	ElectNet
The need to gain access to expertise and/or technology	✓	✓		✓
A desire to improve cost management/cost effectiveness	✓	✓	✓	
A need to bring discipline and control to an in-house function		✓		✓
The need for flexibility in wages and conditions	✓			
A solution to the problem of merging two IT cultures		✓		
The need to adopt a market orientation			✓	
The inability of the existing supplier to service IT needs				✓
The need to create a new IT strategy				✓

The factors listed in Table 3 are not exhaustive of the various motivations that may underlie the decision to outsource, but appear to be representative of those found in prior research. For example, Lacity and Hirschheim (1993) in their study of outsourcing in the IT industry, provide a list of six reasons why organisations may choose to pursue outsourcing (see Table 4). One motivation listed in Table 4, which was not revealed in interviews with managers in the four organisations, is 'reaction to the bandwagon'. This refers to an organisation engaging in outsourcing due to its increasing popularity, or fashion. The degree of publicity that the financial press gives to organisations engaging in large outsourcing contracts may also serve to reinforce the desirability of outsourcing as a 'smart' business solution.

Table 4
Reasons for initiating the outsourcing evaluation (from Lacity and Hirschheim, 1993)

1. Reaction to the efficiency imperative
2. The need to acquire resources
3. Reaction to the bandwagon
4. Reduce uncertainty
5. Eliminate a troublesome function
6. Enhance credibility

Criteria used to evaluate outsourcing decisions

The four firms used a range of criteria to guide their decisions about whether to outsource a particular function, and to whom to outsource to. These are summarised in Tables 5 and 6.

Gradient, Central and Greentrees tended to outsource only those activities that were not considered their core business. ElectNet did not explicitly consider whether it should outsource IT on its formation as a new organisation, as managers saw little choice but to engage outside contractors. Cost performance of the outsourcer was important to all firms, as was the level of expertise and experience of the outsourcer. However, for most firms over the course of the contract period, non-cost concerns came to assume greater prominence. This change in emphasis appears to be a result of the important issues that were not anticipated at the start of the outsourcing relationship but arose during the contract period. Greentrees and Gradient considered the strength of the human resource management and safety practices of the outsourcer, as the outsourcers' employees were working alongside in-house employees. Gradient also focused on the environmental practices and history of potential outsourcers. Greentrees' 'business criteria' were moderated by the philosophical leanings of the council, and a desire to maintain in-house expertise in various areas.

Central considered the outsourcers' approach to strategic planning while ElectNet did not; it intended to keep strategic planning of IT in-house. Both Central and ElectNet considered the ability of the outsourcers to draw on IT expertise from larger corporate resources. All four organisations placed great importance on the outsourcer bringing expertise and skills to the firm, so this was a central criterion.

Table 5
Criteria used to decide which functions to outsource

Criteria	Gradient Steel	Central Energy	Greentrees Council	ElectNet
Core or non-core business	✓	✓	✓	
The ready availability of alternate specialised service providers	✓		✓	
Philosophical considerations of what should be outsourced			✓	
The desire to maintain an in-house expertise			✓	

Table 6
Criteria used to evaluate outsourcing tenders

Criteria	Gradient Steel	Central Energy	Greentrees Council	ElectNet
Expertise, skills and experience of outsourcer/ quality delivery	✓	✓	✓	✓
Financial benefits/cost savings/defined cost reduction paths/billing arrangements	✓	✓	✓	✓
Attention to human resource management/staff transition issues	✓	✓	✓	
Ability of an outsourcer to draw on wider corporate resources		✓		✓
Attention to safety and environmental issues	✓		✓	
Approach to strategic planning of IT		✓		
Plans for managing the contract		✓		

Core competencies and core activities

One of the most difficult aspects of outsourcing decisions is deciding what should, and should not, be outsourced. As stated in Chapter 1, some commentators argue that organisations should outsource activities for which they do not have a critical strategic need or special capabilities, and focus their attention on core competencies. Managers in all but one organisation studied stated (voluntarily) that this was a criterion in the outsourcing decisions. There was agreement, however, that it is difficult to determine those activities that are core competencies, and those that are not.

While none of the managers interviewed believed that core business functions had been outsourced, all four organisations outsourced functions that were critical to their core business operations to varying degrees. In some situations, these were functions for which they did have some expertise. For example, Gradient outsourced the job of collecting and moving scrap between the various areas of the steel processing plant, for reprocessing in the furnace. This process was critical to the steel-making process: scrap made up 20 per cent of the input to the furnace, and any delays in the delivery of skips to the furnace, or quality control problems within the scrap, could lead to the shutting down of the furnace, or to a dangerous accident. However, in the areas of scrap collection, maintenance of cast moulds and the removal and sale of slag, the outsourcers were able to demonstrate clearly that they had a level of expertise and skills that Gradient did not have, and were also able to offer significant cost savings.

Information technology was becoming an increasingly important aspect of the business at both Central and ElectNet. Any interruptions to the service could lead to serious customer service problems. Yet the growing levels of expertise and skills required to support an in-house function were clearly outside the core competencies and capabilities of both of these organisations, and this fact was a prime consideration for outsourcing such an important part of their businesses.

In the road construction and maintenance area of Greentrees, quality control was very important. However, compared to the other three firms, the activities outsourced by Greentrees were far less critical to its core business operations. Interestingly, a lack of expertise or competency was not a prime driver for outsourcing in most areas, as in-house employees were often working on similar projects to that of the outsourced functions.

Benefits of outsourcing

As discussed in Chapter 1, outsourcing can provide a range of benefits. These are summarised in Table 7. Clearly, it is difficult to isolate benefits that result from a specific outsourcing activity, so the list below is probably not complete.

Table 7
Benefits of outsourcing

Benefits	Gradient Steel	Central Energy	Greentrees Council	ElectNet
Access to expertise	✓	✓		
Greater accountability and cost consciousness		✓		✓
Greater discipline in IT planning		✓		✓
Improved service provision		✓		✓
Improvements in control		✓		✓
Benchmarking of internal services			✓	
Opportunity for the firm to focus on priorities			✓	
Operational efficiencies	✓			
Financial benefits	✓			
Flexibility in service provision			✓	
Development of new management skills				✓

Key issues in managing the outsourcing relationship

In Chapter 1, two questions were posed that relate to the management of the outsourcing relationship:

- What are important issues that must be managed within an outsourcing relationship?
- Is it more difficult to control an outsourced activity, compared to an in-house function?

The first question is addressed here. A range of issues emerged within the four organisations, following their outsourcing experiences, which influenced their ability to establish close and co-operative relationships with the outsourcers. These included the following:

- specifications in the contract;
- the transition period and initial expectations;
- managing different cultures;
- communication processes;
- the use of performance measures and incentives;
- managing relationships between the outsourcer and multiple internal customers;
- developing new management skills within the firm;
- building trust between the firm and the outsourcer;
- encouraging higher levels of performance within the firm;
- managing the impact on employees within the firm; and
- managing safety and environmental practices.

The following pages highlight the lessons learned by the four organisations as a result of their outsourcing.

Specifications in the contract

Inadequately specified contracts are cited as a major reason for the failure of some outsourcing relationships, particularly in the information technology area (Robertson, 1998; Domberger, 1998). In each of the four organisations, inadequate specifications in the contract, particularly at the start of the relationship, emerged as a barrier to establishing smooth relationships with the outsourcers.

At Central, these problems related to the ambiguous specification of the baseline services that were included in the fixed payment, and the precise cost that the outsourcers would charge Central for those baseline services. There was also an absence of performance measures in the contract, which had to be renegotiated several years later. Similarly, Gradient found that it took some years to develop appropriate performance measures for the outsourcing agreements.

Gradient identified several limitations that arose from inadequate contract provisions. There were disputes over which party had responsibility for certain costs, such as the cost of replacement of equipment. This problem could have been expected to arise, as many of the outsourcers were sharing facilities with the company. Initially, Gradient contracted for fixed price contracts. However, over time, it began to incorporate flexibility into long-term contracts, so that the firm could benefit from the outsourcers' cost improvements as they occurred.

In the early years of its outsourcing experiences, Greentrees based its outsourcing decisions and contracts primarily on out-of-pocket costs.

However, Greentrees came to include more specific performance expectations in its contracts as it gained greater experience in managing contractors. These service levels included occupational health and safety measures, levels of service delivery, and issues relating to public liability. They also came to include broader cost criteria, including opportunity costs and transaction costs.

Greentrees undertook strict performance reviews of its contractors in areas such as road building and construction, and parks maintenance. In the road building area, this included reviewing the project against the design criteria. Parks maintenance reviews included cost performance and the quality of the service delivered. A unique aspect of the evaluation process was that contractors were assessed against in-house providers.

A common theme that emerged among some of the organisations was the haste with which contracts were negotiated. This clearly helps explain why there was some dissatisfaction with the nature of the provisions of the contracts. However, ElectNet undertook considerable research before venturing into an outsourcing contract; yet managers still found there were aspects of the relationship that were not anticipated, and should have been incorporated into the contract.

Clearly, organisations need to enter contracts that can be revised over time. As the relationship develops, both parties may come to recognise specific needs and requirements, which were difficult to anticipate at the start of the relationship. All four organisations were able to revise their contracts over time, and thus remedy the inadequacies in the initial contracts by incorporating more sophisticated provisions to cover areas such as performance measurement and occupational health and safety, to better assign responsibility for costs, and specify the sharing of cost improvements.

The transition period and initial expectations

As part of the enthusiasm for engaging an outsourcer, some managers had high expectations of achieving distinct improvements in service provision, often within a short time frame. This was certainly the expectation among managers at Central, but those high expectations did not eventuate. There were several reasons for this, including a loss of organisational skills after several valuable IT staff left Central, and conflicts which emerged between the company and the outsourcers because they were working towards different objectives. In addition, it took some time to clarify the contract and the nature of the working relationship.

Similarly, ElectNet suffered some initial difficulties in establishing a smooth relationship with its outsourcers as the handover from the previous suppliers to the outsourcers was only six weeks. Again, important skills were lost to the firm with the exit of the previous suppliers, and the handover time was too limited to convey to the outsourcer the specialised IT knowledge that was needed.

It is very difficult to measure the benefits of outsourcing in the short term, as the introduction of an outsourcer is often accompanied by changes in systems, structures and operations. Introducing an outsourcer into the operations of a firm is likely to involve the outsourcer learning new skills, which may slow improvements in service provision in the short term. In addition, the development of a good working relationship between the outsourcer and an organisation's employees needs time to develop in order to realise those performance improvements.

Managing different cultures

Much has been written about organisational culture and its impact on organisational functioning. Organisational culture can be defined as the shared values, meanings and understandings that are specific to an organisation and underlie how people construct reality and interpret particular events, actions and situations (Morgan, 1986). An organisation's culture encompasses specific knowledge, standard operating procedures and 'ways of doing things' (Langfield-Smith, 1995).

In the case of Central and ElectNet, both companies were former public sector organisations, which outsourced their IT to specialist globalised commercial entities. Given the different origins and nature of the specialisation, it is probably inevitable that the specialist providers would have a different culture to that of the two firms. The issue of cultural differences arose in several areas of the outsourcing relationship.

Central found its IT outsourcer, Global Systems, to be highly commercial and militaristic in its operations, whereas Central itself had recently been formed from two traditional public sector organisations. It was only after eighteen months that these differences began to normalise, as Central came to adopt more commercial principles and Global Systems came to learn 'the Central way'. While ElectNet included in its contracts a requirement for the outsourcers to commit to the vision and values of the company, managers underestimated how difficult it would be to achieve an alignment in which the outsourcer understood how the firm operated, and the values that were driving the business. ElectNet's managers now believe that this issue needs to be considered more explicitly in any future outsourcing contract.

At Greentrees and Gradient, the outsourcers were typically much smaller contractors with far less developed systems and procedures. Greentrees found it difficult to encourage the small outsourcers to pay sufficient attention to occupational, health and safety issues. Gradient also found that practices in the area of industrial relations and safety among the outsourcers differed from that of the firm and believes that more effort needs to be placed on evaluating the values of an outsourcer before entering a contract.

While there is no 'solution' to problems that arise due to cultural differences, an awareness of the issue and its potential impact on the relationship between a firm and an outsourcer can alert both parties to the danger of making too many assumptions about how either party will operate within the new relationship.

Communication processes

Key issues in establishing the protocol for effective communications between the firm and its outsourcers include whether or not there is a single point or multiple points of contact within the firm, and the regularity of formal meetings.

At Central, an important issue was establishing the point of contact to manage the relationship. Initially the IT&T outsourcing manager handled day-to-day problems that emerged between the outsourcer and the various businesses of Central. One manager at Central suggested that while managing the transition, this manager should have focused solely on establishing the relationship, with the day-to-day running of the process being left to subordinates. Regular meetings were held between managers and the outsourcers to review performance and to discuss future plans.

At ElectNet, monthly meetings were held to review performance against service targets. However, the outsourcers established direct relationships with a series of 'systems owners' from a variety of different functions. At Gradient, multiple contact points were also necessary, as there were many different internal customers for the outsourcers.

At Gradient, co-ordination of production required high levels of communication between the outsourcers and the firm. The activities that were outsourced were critical to the core production processes, so any disruption in supply or product quality could affect the smooth running of the business. A period of negotiation was required before the outsourcers could provide seamless supply.

Establishing formal communication protocols is important, particularly early in the relationship with an outsourcer, to help establish the ground rules and expectations of each party. This may involve single or multiple contact points, depending on the characteristics of the function that is being delivered by the outsourcer and the complexity or critical nature of the service.

Performance measures and incentives

The activity of outsourcing highlighted the importance of performance measures and incentives, even when these forms of controls are not used to manage in-house functions.

Both Gradient and Central designed performance measures and targets to provide the most appropriate incentives for the outsourcers to deliver quality services. Gradient was able to build more flexibility into subsequent contracts to allow it to take advantage of performance improvements of outsourcers. Central used a risk/reward scheme to encourage the outsourcer to achieve more profits when undertaking a new project, which also delivered cost savings to Central. These examples emphasise the way in which incentive systems can be structured to benefit both parties in the relationship.

Greentrees undertook strict performance reviews of its contractors in areas such as road building and construction, and parks maintenance. For the road building and construction areas, this included reviewing projects against performance measures that reflected design criteria. For parks maintenance, reviews included cost performance and the quality of the service delivered. At ElectNet, performance was evaluated in terms of systems availability and reliability.

The implementation of performance measures to evaluate and control the work of outsourcers was a common development in the four organisations. It was less common, however, to explicitly tie rewards to the achievement of those performance targets. As suggested in Chapter 1, the legal separation between a firm and its outsourcer may encourage managers to take a close look at control systems, including the implementation of performance measures.

Managing multiple customer relationships

In clarifying the relationship between an organisation and an outsourcer, and achieving more control over the outsourced activity, it is important for an outsourcer to identify who are the internal customers for its service.

At Central, each of the four businesses were the internal customers for the service provided by Global Services, so there were direct contacts between the outsourcer and the four business areas. At Gradient, the relationships were complex, and initially there was some confusion over which areas of the business the outsourcers were servicing. Over time, contractors agreed to the development of KPIs for their individual internal customers. While this was initially difficult for some contractors to accept, it helped clarify what was important in each area, and allowed the outsourcers to direct their efforts towards critical performance areas.

Establishing the form of the customer relationship and the identity of the internal customers is an important part of the communication process. It provides a way of solving problems as they arise, particularly in the early days of a contract, and establishing expectations in relation to service provision.

New management skills

Managers at each of the organisations highlighted the need to develop new management skills as part of the outsourcing process. At Greentrees new skills related to encouraging and training managers to identify market opportunities for outsourcing. This required line managers to scan the market to assess new types of service businesses that were being established, and to determine if they could be utilised in a cost-effective way by the council.

The IT manager at ElectNet acknowledged that new skills had developed to manage the outsourcer, but believed that these skills should not only apply to the outsourcing situation—they were precisely the types of skills that should be applied to manage in-house functions. This leads to the observation that the legal separation between a firm and its outsourcer seems to highlight the importance of management and control issues in the eyes of some managers. Managers at both Central and ElectNet alluded to this issue, stating that the existence of a 'real' monetary relationship between the two parties (as opposed to one involving internal transfer pricing) led to an increase in control.

Establishing co-operative relationships with outsourcers and their staff may require managers to develop new skills in many areas, including communication and negotiation. In addition, the outsourcing of a function may require managers to learn how to relate to former staff who may now work for an outsourcer, but nevertheless be performing essentially the same functions as before the outsourcing took place.

Building high levels of trust

It has been claimed that a high level of trust is important for establishing a close co-operative relationship between a firm and its outsourcer, and even for establishing a workable contract (Langfield-Smith and Greenwood, 1998; Domberger, 1998).

An awareness of the need to build high levels of trust between the firm and the outsourcer emerged in all four companies. Managers at Central felt that developing trust was the most difficult part of outsourcing the IT function, and that elements of distrust arose between Central and the outsourcer, largely because of inadequacies in the contract. Moreover, it was suggested by one manager that the mere existence of a contract could create an element of mistrust.

At Central, some mistrust initially arose when managers within the four businesses were charged by the outsourcer for their use of IT services. This action was met with suspicion and claims of overcharging. The reaction was a result of the transition towards 'realistic' charging for IT services, which had not been fully explained to managers. Clearly, effective communication may provide a way to encourage the development of trust, by clarifying expectations and encouraging repeated positive interactions.

Encouraging higher levels of internal performance

There were several ways that the engagement of an outsourcer led to improved performance levels in the firm.

At Greentrees, outsourcing provided a method for assessing the performance of internal service providers. For example, in road construction and maintenance, and parks maintenance, the performance of internal employees was benchmarked against the outsourcers in terms of cost and quality of service. Thus, outsourcing resulted in performance improvements for several areas of the council.

At Central, new practices introduced as part of the outsourcing encouraged greater cost management and accountability in the four businesses. Before the outsourcing of IT, there had been little control over the businesses' use of IT services. After outsourcing, each business was required to justify any requirements for IT development as part of the annual IT budget, and was charged for its usage of IT services. This provided an incentive for managers to consider carefully their requirements and the way in which they were utilising information technology within their businesses. A similar situation existed at ElectNet where a greater degree of accountability for IT development emerged following the outsourcing of the IT function.

As mentioned in earlier sections in this chapter, it appears that improved controls can result from the outsourcing of an activity. In the case of the organisations studied, this resulted from increased levels of accountability of internal business functions, and increased performance outcomes due to benchmarking against the outsourcers.

The impact on employees

The impact on employees within a firm must be considered carefully in the face of increased outsourcing. Outsourcing an in-house function may result in employees leaving the firm, gaining employment with the outsourcer, or being transferred to other functions within the firm, and adverse reactions of employees to outsourcing may influence the effective management of the relationship. At Gradient, the firm worked with the outsourcers to manage the conditions under which the outsourcer offered jobs to displaced employees.

At Central, there was some concern among IT staff who had chosen to be redeployed within the firm. This was managed carefully, so as not to spread unrest throughout the organisation. Indeed, one of the criteria considered by Central when choosing between various tenderers was how the outsourcers planned to manage transitional issues for staff.

Another important consideration is that outsourced staff may be employed under different conditions to those of in-house staff, and this may lead to some dissatisfaction. When the outsourcers' employees worked alongside the firm's employees, at Gradient and Greentrees, issues of equity in pay and working conditions became important in achieving a harmonious relationship. In addition, as a firm engages in increased outsourcing, employees may experience anxiety, as they see a reduction in the in-house labour force.

At Gradient, managers acknowledged that one of the difficulties that had to be managed in the early days of outsourcing, was that the outsourcers' employees were employed under different industrial relations conditions, as compared to Gradient's employees. In later contracts, an outsourcer's industrial relations approaches were considered specifically in the tender evaluation process, in order to minimise any inequities or disquiet among employees.

It is difficult to anticipate the impact of outsourcing on employees that remain with a firm, whether they are those employees that are redeployed as a result of the outsourcing or those that consider there to be inequities that have arisen with the introduction of outsourcing. The management of employee transitions should be included as a formal part of the outsourcing plan, and it may be the responsibility of both the firm and the outsourcer.

Safety and environment practices

When an activity has been outsourced, a firm may be responsible for the occupational health and safety of the outsourcers' employees, and the environmental practices associated with the outsourced activity.

At Gradient, it was important to evaluate the safety practices and environmental values of potential outsourcers in the initial assessment. There were serious ramifications for this organisation if an outsourcer was not sufficiently safety conscious, in terms of both human safety and potential disruptions to processing. This was difficult to implement if left until after a contract was finalised. Gradient assisted its outsourcers in gaining skills in this area by including the outsourcers' employees in its in-house training programs.

Greentrees came to realise the importance of contractors observing occupational health and safety standards, and worked hard to convince contractors to comply with minimum standards. At Central and ElectNet these concerns did not arise, probably because of the low safety and environmental risk associated with the outsourced functions.

It is not difficult for a firm to ignore the safety and environmental practices of the outsourcers. However, legal and moral responsibilities clearly need to be considered. In areas where there are high risks for occupational health and safety and environmental management, the organisation's expectations should be shared with the outsourcers, and in-house training programs may be opened up to outsourcers' employees.

Summary

In this section, eleven issues have been identified as important in the management of close and co-operative relationships between an organisation and its outsourcers. An emerging theme is that outsourcing can provide the means to achieving greater control within the organisation. In the next section, the control implications of outsourcing will be explored in greater detail.

The impact of outsourcing on control

A frequently cited disadvantage of outsourcing is a loss of control over knowledge, skills, and processes. The potential for this loss of control may depend on the nature of the function that is outsourced. Outsourcing some functions, for example cleaning and catering, would not entail a high risk of loss of skills or knowledge for most firms. Outsourcing other activities, such as those in the areas of product design, manufacturing processing or information technology, are more likely to lead to a loss of knowledge and skills, and possibly to a loss of control over those functions. The evidence relating to this issue in the four cases is ambiguous. In two of the organisations (Central Energy and ElecNet) managers believed that control, in terms of accountability for the activity, increased as a result of outsourcing. Safeguarding against a loss of skills and knowledge was a minor consideration for Greentrees and Gradient.

Improvements in control and accountability

Although Central did not seek control through financial means, there was a variety of mechanisms that served to create control in its relationship with Global Services. These were through specifications within the contract; the building of trust between the firm and the outsourcer; the implementation of performance measures and incentives schemes; and the implementation of greater accountability systems within the firm.

In contrast to the criticism that outsourcing can lead to a loss in control, Central engaged in outsourcing as a way of improving control over IT activities and the cost of IT. When IT was performed in-house, management found it difficult to exercise effective control over spending by businesses within Central, and to control new product development by IT staff. The internal transfer pricing systems did not work to create a cost consciousness among buying and selling parties. The corporate boundary between Central and Global Services essentially created a 'control barrier'. It could be argued that cost centres and profit centres are created to effect the same type of outcomes. The control advantages of this form of internal structuring, however, did not seem to work within Central prior to outsourcing. We can only speculate why this was the case:

- Was it too difficult to impose more effective control through an internal pricing mechanism?
- Were the relationships between Central employees too close to allow for the implementation of effective control?
- Was outsourcing the only solution that could have been applied to improve the control situation?

At Central, new practices introduced as part of the outsourcing encouraged greater cost management and accountability among the four businesses. Before the outsourcing of IT, there had been little control over the businesses' use of IT services. After outsourcing, they were required to justify any requirements for IT development as part of the annual IT budget, and were charged for their usage of IT services. This provided an incentive for managers to carefully consider their requirements and the way in which they were utilising information technology within their business. Managers at both Central and ElectNet stated that the outsourcer brought more discipline to the IT process.

At ElectNet, similar issues arose. 'Excessive' IT developments were curbed with the engagement of the IT outsourcer, as managers found they were invoiced for new IT development. Greater accountability for IT costs ensued.

At Greentrees, various functions were performed by both in-house employees and outsourcer employees, which led to an increase in efficiency among the firm's employees, through the use of benchmarking as a standard against which the firm's employees were assessed.

All four companies implemented both formal and informal controls to manage their relationships with outsourcers. Formal controls included performance measures, financial incentive systems, regular meetings, and systems for increased accountability over the use of the outsourcers' services. In some cases, it appeared that these control systems were more rigorous than those used within the firms to control in-house activities. There may be a perception that stronger systems are needed to counter the potential loss of control that might occur when outsourcing a function to an outside supplier. However, a manager at ElectNet stated that the systems being used to manage the IT outsourcers were the same types of systems that should be used to manage in-house functions (but were not). The question remains: Was outsourcing the only solution to improving control over internal functions? Perhaps it was the easiest solution.

Retaining knowledge and skills

One of the criteria that Greentrees applied when deciding which activities should be outsourced was that it wished to retain its expertise or intellectual investment in a particular area. This arose from the realisation that unless knowledge and skills were retained in certain areas, it might be difficult to bring a function back in-house. Thus, at Greentrees, many services were undertaken by both in-house and outsourced employees.

Gradient was also sensitive about retaining its technical expertise following outsourcing, and was conscious of the potential risk of dependency when tied to an outsourcer. If there was only a single firm that offered a particular service, and the chance of losing its technical skills through outsourcing, then the company did not want to enter into such a relationship with an outsourcer.

For Central and ElectNet, the issue of losing skills and knowledge was not as relevant. Both companies outsourced the IT functions, as they did not believe that it was possible, or desirable, to build up in-house expertise in the area. While Central had strong capabilities in IT before the outsourcing, the benefits that would accrue from gaining the specialised expertise of the outsourcer were greater than any risk of exposure or dependence as the result of a loss of skills.

Importantly, both Central and ElectNet retained ownership of the IT hardware and software. Managers in both companies stated that this was the key to retaining some control over the IT function, and safeguarding against any undue dependency on the outsourcer.

Is it more difficult to control an outsourced function?

Is it more difficult to control an outsourced activity, compared to an in-house function?

The legal separation between an outsourcer and a firm may lead managers to believe that there is a need for greater control. It may also mean that control can only be achieved in limited ways. Direct supervision over staff and operations will not usually be possible, so greater reliance must be placed on formal (indirect) control mechanisms. Compared to the processes involved in implementing in-house controls, more negotiations will take place between a firm and an outsourcer when controls are changed, or when new controls are imposed. Cultural differences between a firm and outsourcer may make it difficult to implement formal control and to encourage the growth of informal controls.

This does not necessarily mean, however, that control will be weaker. It seems that the discipline of having to specify the nature of the service before going to tender may force a firm to specify for the first time its precise service needs, which may allow it to more easily develop performance measures and other controls over the service provided (Domberger, 1998). Also, by retaining ownership over various key assets, firms may safeguard against creating situations of over-dependency on an outsourcer.

In conclusion, it is important to note that none of the managers in the four organisations stated that control was more difficult under outsourcing, and managers in two firms believed that control had been strengthened following outsourcing.

Conclusion

This report has focused on the outsourcing experiences of four Australian firms. It was not unexpected that several differences would be found, as the firms covered different industries, and had different degrees of experience with outsourcing. The management of the outsourcing relationship was an important focus of the study, as was the consideration of control issues associated with an outsourced function. It seems that conventional notions of a loss of control following outsourcing may not hold. In the case of at least two of the firms studied, control increased, due to the implementation of systems that were stricter than those that had existed before the function was outsourced. Clearly further studies could be undertaken to see whether this is the more general rule.

BIBLIOGRAPHY

Alexander M and Young D 'Strategic Outsourcing', *Long Range Planning*, 29 (1), 1996, pp. 116–119.

Australian Government, *Commonwealth Competitive Neutrality Policy Statement*, Canberra, 1996.

Banaghan M 'The Best Way to Keep Staff: Let Them Go', *Business Review Weekly*, 9 October 1995.

Bendor-Samuel P *Managing for Success*, Everest Group, Inc., 1996.

Chalos P 'Costing, Control, and Strategic Analysis in Outsourcing Decisions'. *Journal of Cost Management*, Winter 1995, pp. 31–37.

Domberger S *The Contracting Organisation: A Strategic Guide to Outsourcing*, New York: Oxford University Press, 1998.

Domberger S and Farago S 'Competitive Tendering and the Performance of Government Trading Enterprises in NSW', Graduate School of Business Working Paper Series 01–94, University of Sydney, 1994.

Drtina RE 'The Outsourcing Decision', *Management Accounting*, March 1994, pp. 56–62.

Eroglu D 'Global or Domestic Outsourcing of the 'IS' Function: Implications and Recommendations', in Zahra SA and Ali A. (eds) *The Impact of Innovation and Technology in the Global Marketplace*, New York, International Business Press, 1994.

Hamel G and Prahalad CK *Competing for The Future*. Boston: Harvard University Press, 1994.

Grabner G *The Embedded Firm*, London: Routledge, 1993.

Lacity MC and Hirschheim R *Information Systems Outsourcing*, Chichester, John Wiley and Sons, 1993.

Lacity MC, Willcocks LP and Feeny DF 'IT Outsourcing: Maximise Flexibility and Control', *Harvard Business Review*, May–June 1995, pp. 84–93.

Langfield-Smith K 'Organisational Culture and Control', in Berry AJ, Broadbent J and

Otley D *Management Control; Theories, Issues and Practices*, London; Macmillan Press, 1995, pp. 179–200.

Langfield-Smith K and Greenwood M 'Developing Cooperative Supplier Partnerships: A Case Study of Toyota', *Journal of Management Studies*, 35(3), 1998, pp. 331–353.

Long S 'Companies by name only', *The Australian Financial Review*, 16 April 1998, Special Report: Outsourcing, 1–2.

Lorenzoni G and Baden-Fuller C 'Creating a Strategic Center to Manage a Web of Partners', *California Management Review*, 27 (3), 1995, pp. 146–163.

McFarlan FW and Nolan RL 'How to Manage an IT Outsourcing Alliance', *Sloan Management Review*, Winter 1995, pp. 9–23.

McHugh P. Merli G and Wheeler WA *Beyond Business Process Reengineering*, Chichester, John Wiley and Sons, 1995.

Morgan G *Images of Organisation*, London: Sage, 1986.

Plunkett S 'Calling in the Experts', *Business Review Weekly*, 9 October 1995, pp. 92–96.

Quinn JB *Intelligent Enterprise: A Knowledge and Service Based Paradigm for Industry*, New York, Free Press, 1992.

Quinn JB and Hilmer FG 'Strategic Outsourcing', *Sloan Management Review*, Summer 1994, pp. 43–55.

Rimmer SJ 'Competitive Tendering and Contracting: Theory and Research', *The Australian Economic Review*, 3rd Quarter 1994, pp. 79–85.

Robertson R 'Contract details are the secret to success', *The Australian Financial Review*, 16 April 1998, Special Report: Outsourcing, 5.

Rotary B and Robertson I *The Truth About Outsourcing*, Aldershot, Gower, 1995.

Syvret S 'Financial sector putting more work outside', *The Australian Financial Review*, 16 April 1998, Special Report: Outsourcing, 12.

Walker G and Weber D 'A Transaction Cost Approach to Make-or-Buy Decisions', *Administrative Science Quarterly*, 29, 1984, pp. 373–391.